THIAGARAJA
A GREAT MUSICIAN SAINT

(1759-1847)

(WITH SARGAM NOTATION)

M. S. RAMASWAMI AIYAR

GYAN

Published by

GYAN

Gyan Publishing House
5, Ansari Road
Daryaganj, New Delhi-110002
Phone: 011-47034999, 9811692060
E-mail: books@gyanbooks.com

Distribution Network
gyanbooks.com
India, USA, Canada, UK, Australia, France

ISBN : 978-81-212-4093-2 (PB)
First Published, 1927

2nd Impression 2020

Printed at: Gyan Press, Delhi.

THIAGARAJA
A GREAT MUSICIAN SAINT
(1759-1847)

PREFACE

Between 1921 and 1923, my "Thiagaraja" appeared in the *Hindu* and *Everymans Review*; and I thank their respective Editors therefor. Early in 1925, it was delivered as a Lecture before the Fourth All India Music Conference at Lucknow. In 1926, it was re-written, enlarged, and even divided into chapters. And on Friday, July 2, 1926, in its modified form, it was delivered as a Lecture, along with other ones, at Mysore under the auspices of its University.

The appreciation wherewith it was welcomed by the audiences of Lucknow and Mysore (and also of Bangalore where the lecture was repeated); the ovation wherewith it was greeted elsewhere by my friends and other eminent persons; and last, not least, the princely donation wherewith His Highness the Maharaja of Mysore, rightly designated by the Hon'ble Mr. Justice V. V. Srinivasa Iyengar as "Dakshina Janaka," encouraged me;—all jointly and severally contributed to the publication of my "Thiagaraja", in regular book form.

How I came to write this book is told at length in my Introduction.

I avail myself of this opportunity to record here my heartfelt thanks to Mr. V. Subrahmanya Iyer, B.A., Fellow of the Mysore University and Retired Registrar of the University of Mysore, for the kindness wherewith he went through the proof-sheets and even otherwise gave me very valuable suggestions ; to Messrs. Solden & Co. of Madras for the excellent Blocks they gave me to illustrate the book with ; and to Mr: D. Sundara Varadan of Everymans Press, Madras, for the attention and care wherewith he executed the printing of this work; never mind the few typographical errors inevitable to the first Edition of any book, especially when the author and the printer are about 300 miles apart from each other.

It only remains for me to say that any hints and suggestions for the improvement of the book will be thankfully received.

I must, however, mention that the few characters, that appear in this book, invariably spoke in the Vernacular. Since this biography has been written in English, I must forewarn my reader that, while the thoughts alone belong to those characters, the language is entirely mine.

COIMBATORE
Wednesday October 5, 1927. } *M. S. Ramaswami Aiyar.*

DEDICATED

WITH PERMISSION TO

H. H. SRI KRISHNARAJA WADIYAR BAHADUR IV
G.C.S.I., G.B.E.,
MAHARAJA OF MYSORE.

One of the greatest Patrons of Fine Arts, especially,

MUSIC

both Eastern and Western,

but for whose generous support and gracious
encouragement this humble work
could not have been published.

NOTE.

My feelings of gratitude compel me to inscribe here the three Songs which I composed in honor of His Highness the Maharaja of Mysore and sang before him.

I. A New Sankarabharana Varnam.

N.B.—This Varnam contains a Benediction in the former part and a History of Indian Music in the latter—the whole thing being wound up with an Appeal that the greatest Karnatic King should raise back the Karnatic Music to the pinnacle of its former glory. His Highness graciously responded to the Appeal and enabled me to publish my "Thiagaraja" with a munificent grant. For the Varnam, see pp. 224—226.

II. A New Mohana Varnam.

N.B.—This was intended to commemorate the celebration of the Silver Jubilee, on Monday, August 8, 1927, of His Highness's most successful Reign. The Varnam is as follows :—

Mohana Raga] **Pallavi.** [Ata Thala

मोहनांगि मोहनरते श्री चामुण्डादेवि.

Anupallavi.

पाहिसर्वदा श्रीमहीशूरपुराधीश श्रीकृष्णराज—
राजेन्द्रं भक्तवत्सलेसुवरदेवरसुरार्चितांघ्रिपंकजे.

Swaras.	Sahithyam.
गा-धपगारि-सरि-धधसा—	ओमितिवरपंजरशुकि—
पाधप-धासध-सारिंस-री—	सर्वतन्त्रात्मिकेसिद्धिप्रदे—
गापग-पाधप-धासंध-सां—	सर्वशक्त्यात्मिकेमोक्षप्रदे—
संधप-गारि-सारि ;	अभयकारि-रमे ;
गग-धपगारि-गधपग-रिगपा—	कनककशिपुवरसुतप्रोके—
पग-पधसंधप-धसंधपग-रिगस —	नखमुखसुखरितवीणावाय—
पप्प-पगसरि-धध्ध-धपगपा—	सुस्वरानुभवभृंगीनिभे—
संस्सं-संध ;	चारुतर ;
धसां-संरीं-रिंगां-पंगारिं—	दिव्यरत्नांबरे मंजुल—
संरिंगपंगारिं-संगंरीं-रिंगसं—	वाग्विलासे -वन्दे-सुंदर—
संरिंध-धसंप-पधग—	तरवदने-चंद्रदि—
पधसं-संधप-गधप-गारि-सध—	नमणिनयने-शमनगर्वनि—
सरि-गगपा ;	ग्रहसुप्रिये ;
धधध-रिंरिंरिं-धध-रिंरिं—	सुमधुरतरसुवचने—
धरिंरिं-संधप-गारिस-सरिग—	सकलजनहृत्सदन अतिर—
पधसां-संरिंसां-धपं-धसंधा—	सगुणे-अरुणारुण-चरणांबुज—
पग-पधपागारि-गपगारिस—	करुणामृत-वरुणालये—
गपधसध (मो)	शुभमंगल— (मो)

Charanam.

सारसलोचनयुगले समस्तमंगलभोगदेनमोऽस्तुते.

Swaras.		Sahithyam.	
1. सां-धसंधपा-गधपगारि—		1. सादरमव-त्रिपुरसुंदरि—	
सरिस-सरिगपधसां—		शिवे-भक्तसुलभे-सं—	
सरिगपध ;	(सा)	गीतप्रिये ;	(सा)
2. पाधप-गप-गगारिस—		2. मंजुलगुणगणरते—	
रीगारि--सारि-गपगारि—		रंजनिसकलदुरित—	
गापधं-सध-पगरिग—		भंजनिशंकारिनि—	
धासंरिं-गांरिं-संध—		रंजनिनवमणि—	
गांरिंसं-रींसंध-सांधप—		सिंजिते--व्यंजित-रंजित—	
धापग-पध—	(सा)	कुंजरगते ;	(सा)
3. धाध-धाध-पधसंधप—		3. देहिदेहि-धर्मार्थकामं—	
गरिस धाध-धाध-सरिगसस—		देहिदेहि-विश्वकारि—	
रिगपारीरि-गपधगग—		णीत्वमेव-श्रीमदाम—	
पधसंपप-धसंरिंधध—		दासपूज्य-पादपद्मे—	
संधंसं-धधसां-गंरिंगंसां—		शरणंशरणं-भास्वरे—	
संधसंपा-गारिगसा—		प्रोज्वले-विश्रुते—	
पधसारि-गपधसं-गंरिंगां—		वरमुनिवंदितचरणे—	
पंगांरिं-संधसंरिं-गंरींसं—		सुरादिनुते-अतिविराजि—	
धपधसं-रिंसांध—		तसुतनो-परात्परे—	
रगपध ;	(सा)	अंब—	(सा)

4. सां-रिगंरिंर-संरिंसंसं—

धपधा-पधसं-संधप—

गधपधा-संधप-गारिस—

पगा-गधपाप-संधा-धरिंसांसं—

रिंसंध-पध ;

संरिं-गंरींरिं-धसंरिं-सांसं—

पग-धापगारिस-धप,सध—

रिस, गरि, पग, धप, संधसां—

सांरिंगंपं-गांरिं-संगंरिं-संधसां—

रिंधसां-पंधंसां-गंरिं, गंसं,

रिंध, संध-रिंसं, रिंध, संध, संप—

गग, पप, धंधं, संसं-गप-धसंधा—

सरिगप-धरिंरिं-धसंसं-पधध—

गपपं-धरिं-धासं-पाध—

गाप-रीग-सगरि—

गपध-गरीं-संधप-गरिस—

गपध-सांरिंगां-गंगं-गंरिंरिंसं—

रिगप-धसंरीं-रिंरिं-रिंसंसंध—

सरिग-पध ; (सा)

4. शांतिनिलयं-देव्यभिष—

कायचामुण्ड्यचलस्था—

किंचन-मानव—

सुखायचतद्गिरिमस्तकंकाव—

रिजल-मुप ;

नेहुंवारियन्त्रजाल—

प्रतिष्ठापनसुचतुरै—निरु—

पमसिल्वर्ज्जमिलिसमये—

अतिरमणीयकल्याणगुणे—

शुभचंद्रमुखि-मनसिज—

रिपुप्रिये-मतंगमुनिकन्यके—

मणिमण्डितसुचरणे-गौरि—

भगवति-सकल-सुजन-हृदय—

सुखदे-नवरत्नपीटसुस्थिते—

पंचास्यसुप्रिये सदा नित्यकल्याणि—

अवनवनवागाररथ्यो—

पवनरचनेरतं श्रीकृष्णं—

अवनिपतिं ; (सा)

III. A New Vanaspathi Krithi.

N.B.—This was composed, as acknowledged in the Krithi itself, at the instance of His Highness. Thereby hangs a tale; and I cannot but tell it. On the night of the 5th July 1926 it was, that I sáng, before the august presence of His Highness the Maharaja of Mysore, the first-mentioned Sankarabharana Varnam. It was followed by a few Krithis of Thiagaraja's. Soon an interesting conversation ensued—which opened my eyes and enabled me to discover that the Maharaja of Mysore was a rare and accomplished scholar, deep philosopher, practised yogi, practical seer, keen administrator, wise ruler, and above all musical genius. I then repeated within myself the following well-known lines :—

"By Nature's gifts ordained mankind to rule
He, like a Titian, formed his brilliant school
And taught congenial spirits to excel
While from his lips impressive wisdom fell."

I was not, however, allowed to muse in this manner. For, suddenly and quite unexpectedly, His Highness put me a question: "*Have you composed any song in any of the* 40 *Extraordinary Ragas*?" O! that Query has had the magical effect of concreting my latent desire to enter into that Reserved Field. The following Vanaspathi Krithi was the result; and so have I stated in Anupallavi: "this (Vanaspathi Krithi) is the direct result of your Highness's Query."

Vanaspathi Raga] Pallavi. [Adi Thala

कृष्णराजराजेन्द्र—श्री

Anupallavi.

कृष्णसन्निभगानलोल
भवताप्रचोदितकार्यमिदम्

Charanam.

मखिचक्रचत्वारिंशद्विषय
सुखिनामाद्यद्विरिसंयुत
वनस्पतिंवंदे श्रीराम
दासोऽहंसुखायजनानाम्

Flourish.

गम—पधानध—पमगार—गा ;
गम—गमपम—पधनिसं—संरिं—सं॑निध—
पधनिसांरि—मपधनीसं—गमपधानिं—
संनिधनिधप—धनिसां ;
निसंमंरि—रिंसंसंनि—धनिंरीं—
संनिरिंसं—संनिनिध—पमगा—
नीसंरि—गामप—धनिसं रीं—
संनि--धनिसं—संनिध—संनिधप—
मगरिस ; (कृ)

OPINIONS

The late Mr. T. V. Seshagiri Aiyar, High Court Judge of Madras, wrote to me on 9-10-24:—

Nothing that I can say can add to the excellence of your *Thiagaraja.* You have done real service to music by the compilation and you have placed the great musician (Thiagaraja) in a light which shows how brilliant a star he is in the musical firmament. I was particularly interested in the careful Judgment you passed on the development of his religious faith. All devotees are fanatics at start. The mellowing influence comes from His Grace late in life. That is why our ancients attached so much importance to Saguna Upasana. It is the road to Nirguna Devotion and Jivan Mukthi itself. Thiagaraja's career is an excellent illustration of this travail of the pious soul. His intolerance showed the acme of his devotion to Sri Rama. He next realised that all devotions lead to the path of salvation. His final discovery was the oneness of many faiths. His songs attest to this gradual unfolding of his spiritual temperament. I find in your book many of the explanations I had heard from the two Umayapuram Brothers regarding the origin and immediate occasion of the Krithis. I have nothing but admiration for the work you have accomplished. The music in me is different from the music in you. I hanker after it and you are full of it. Both of us love it; that is where you and I meet. I hope your efforts may obtain that recognition from the public which your knowledge and scholarship deserve."

Mr. Dilip Kumar Roy, a Music Gritic of Calcutta, wrote to me on 16-10-24:—

"Your book on Thiagaraja gave me great pleasure. As books of this kind are likely to contribute much to the creation and permeation of our interest in Indian Music, I welcome such publications with all my heart. Your spirit of research as well as the elaborate pains you have taken for collecting materials for the book deserve the highest appreciation, specially because of the sad neglect of our intelligentsia of our glorious heritage of music. The book shows how much you love our art. Indeed our art is sure to be recognised by the world in the near future and books such as yours are more than likely to go far towards paving the way for such recognition. Some of the ancedotes of Thiagaraja are elevating reading; and they lend an insight into the personality of the great artist. His attitude towards life is a lofty one; and I feel proud to claim the liver of such a life for one of our musicians."

Rev. H. A. Popley B. A., of Y.M.C.A. wrote to me on 8-11-24 :—

"I have had the pleasure of reading through your work on Thiagaraja. It is a most interesting book and you have brought together a great number of facts and incidents which go to make the man's career most interesting and the story a vivid one. The music-loving public should certainly be thankful to you for the care you have taken. It has helped me very much to understand something of Thiagaraja's life. Before this I was not able to get hold of very much about him; and I am truly grateful to you."

Dr. Sir. Brajendra Nath Seal, M.A., Ph. D., D. Sc., Vice-Chancellor of the University of Mysore, wrote to me on 4-8-26 :—

"Your lectures on South Indian Music (which included *Thiagaraja*) delivered at the Mysore

University on the University extension platform, I am glad to tell you, have been very well received not only by the general public but also by lovers and students of music. Your style of presentation is indeed 'musical' and quite in keeping with your theme. The country must be grateful to you for your labour of love in carrying out this active propaganda."

Mr. K. S. Ramaswami Sastri, B.A., B.L., Sub-Judge, (now, District Judge) Tanjore, wrote to me on 25—8—27 :—

"I have perused with great pleasure and profit the excellent book by Mr. M. S. Ramaswami Aiyar on the great musical composer and saintly devotee of South India—*Thiagaraja*, If India, during the time of her national humiliation and eclipse, was kept alive by the warmth and brightness and vivifying power of the Hindu religion; it is no less true that Hinduism, in its turn, was kept alive by the warmth and brightness and vivifying power of the musician-saints of India. These alone democratised our religion and brought its solace and strength and spirituality to the doors of the people. Of these musician-saints, none is greater or holier and has a greater hold on the popular heart and imagination than Thiagaraja. He was a devotee of

Sri Rama as his Ishta Devata but he revered all glorious aspects of Godhead. He was the most talented, musical genius known in India and yet he was so humble and mellow that he recognised and revered genius in all quarters. He was poor in regard to worldly goods but scorned to sell his soul for wealth.

Mr. Ramaswami Aiyar is himself a musician and an expert in the theory and practice of music and is also a devotee and a public worker. He has hence a special fitness to undertake such a great work as the biography of the prince of musicians and lovers of God. The work has waited for him; and he has waited and equipped himself for the work all his life. Discriminating and critical study, insight, and temperamental kinship are of the essence of a biographer's equipment; and these are possessed by Mr. Ramaswami Aiyar in an abundant measure He has also the gifts of a charming manner and vivid presentation and arresting style. The result is an excellent work on a great man and a great theme.

The special graces of Indian music lie in its melody and its subtlety of graces and its sprituality. It has a wonderful science of its own which has been developed in the course of many centuries from the time of Bharata's *Natya Sastra* The entire treasury of graces, which Indian music had, is found in Thiagaraja and he added to it in abundance from the inner kingdom of his soul. Thiagaraja's songs themselves show the evolution of his devotion to God and his charity and affection towards man! He had his share of trials and troubles in life; but they never dulled the edge of his purity or lessened the glow of his love and devotion. I am not competent to judge about the author's exposition of Thiagaraja's great contribution to the cause of Indian music; but I realise that it is of signal value. Even a man who has no harmony in himself and is not moved with concord of sweet sounds—a man who feels like Dr. Johnson that a music is a kind of noise—cannot but feel the sweet flow of measured sound in Thiagaraja's songs and hymns, the divine touches of emotional sweetness in them, and the mellifluous flow of his words in that most musicial of Indian Vernaculars—the Telugu tongue. He freed music from the fetters of words and at the same time gave to words the wings of harmony. He sounded all the deeps of sound and revelled in his wonderful discoveries of tune and time. Who can follow this adventurous soul sailing unchartered seas of sound, unless he be a musician and a devotee and a lover of humanity? Mr. Ramaswami Aiyar is such a man; and that is why his work is so valuable and excellent. I wish his work ever-increasing public appreciation and regard and hope and wish that he will give us soon an authoritative work on the Rise and Growth of the Music of India."

Mr. N. S. Subba Rao, M. A., Bar-at-Law, Director of Public Instruction, Mysore, wrote to me from Bangalore on 14-9-27 :—

"I return with apologies for the delay the proofs of your forthcoming work on Thiagaraja. I have had time just to skim througn the pages; and I must congratulate you on a valuable piece of work."

CONTENTS

Chapter	Subject	Page
I.	Introduction	1
II.	Thiagaraja's Early Life and Education ...	11
III.	His Date	26
IV.	His Initiation into Music	32
V.	His Battle of Life	37
VI.	His Age	47
VII.	His Spirit	52
VIII.	His Appearance and Characteristics ...	62
IX.	Periods of his Career	70
X.	His Views of Music	95
XI.	His Works on Music	99
XII.	His Signal Service	109
XIII.	His Style and Diction	124
XIV.	His Raga and Thala Systems... ...	130
XV.	His Instruments of Music	140
XVI.	His Contemporaries	144
XVII.	His Philosophy	152
XVIII.	Conclusion	176
Appendix—Sargam Notation		179

THIAGARAJA.

CHAPTER I.

INTRODUCTION.

THIAGARAJA! A great name. Great as, if not greater than, that of Handel or Beethoven or even Tansen. India—especially South India—knows and loves him well. Perhaps too well. In reply to an address presented by the people of Tanjore, during one of his tours, His Highness the Maharaja of Travancore, Visakam Thirunal (1880 to 1885) observed: "I rejoice that I stand to-day on the soil that has produced Appayya Dikshithar and Thiagaraja." Reader! attend a music party in South India and the Sangitha Vidwan will electrify you with Thiagaraja's Krithis *; enter a marriage house and the blooming bride will enchant you with Thiagaraja's Kirthanas; join

* For explanation of Krithis and other terms—see my *Forms of Music*.

a Bhajana Goshti and the devoted Bhaktha will treat you with Thiagaraja's Divyanamavalis ; get into a transit carriage and you will hear your fellow-passengers hum the same Thiagaraja's songs on the highway; *or* go even to a bazar street and you will find the self-same Thiagaraja's snatches greeting you again, though now from a beggar. Thus, from the erudite expert down to the veriest tyro and from the ruling prince down to the lowliest beggar, Thiagaraja has been invariably an entertaining philosopher, friend, and guide.

Even the Europeans and other foreigners would have long ago got to know him, but for the regrettably misleading negligence of some erratic missionaries, the chief of whom was Abbe Dubois. The ambitious author of *The Hindu Manners, Customs and Ceremonies* was—be it noted—a contemporary of Thiagaraja ; for, he lived from 1765 to 1848 and (what is more ?) resided in India from 1792 to 1823. Again, the place of his residence was, neither so far as Peshawar in North West India *nor* Shillong in North East India but very near Thiagaraja—Seringapatam. Hence, he, who proposed to convey to Europe and elsewhere a historic perspective of Hindu Music, amidst other things, ought to have the assurance of his information made doubly sure by original research and direct observation, but not by mere studies in his closet, however indefatigable they might be.

Let me not here be misunderstood that I proceed to dilute the unstinted praise lavished on him by Prof. Max Muller *or* the unrestricted respect paid to him by the Duke of Wellington. That is not my present purpose; nor is it my purpose to criticise his book as a whole. But so far as his music portion is concerned, I emphatically assert that it is a complete travesty of facts, even which I would, full fain, pass over, if it did not lead the way for foreigners to seriously misunderstand Hindu Music.

While, as I shall show in these pages, Thiagaraja left a vast legacy to his successors and rendered national service by considerably altering or extending the scope and possibilities of Hindu Music and preventing it from being drowned in the boisterous ocean of musical technique; the idol of the Duke of Wellington and Prof. Max Muller, shut up by the waters of the Cauvery, chose to rather listen to the insipid chirping of the poor grass-hoppers of the island than cross the river and avail himself of the festive carol of Thiruvaiyar's nightingale; delighted himself in the moonshine of fiction and wrote in the plenitude of his ignorance : "Hindu Music to-day (that is, in the time of Thiagaraja) is the same as it has always been and has undergone no alteration. The charming art is in its infancy. The Hindus are no further advanced in it now than they were two or three thousand years ago." While, as a matter of fact, Indian Music did move from the stage of its "infancy" and develop itself through such stages as, for instance, Bharatha's *Natya-sasthra* of the 6th century, Sharangadev's *Sangitha-ratnakara* of the 13th century, Lochanakavi's *Raga-tharangani* of the 14th century, Pundarika Vittala's *Sadraga-chandrodaya* of the 16th century, Venkatamakhi's *Chathurdandiprakasika* of the 17th century, Muhammad Rezza's *Nagmut-e-Asaphi* of the 19th century, and Bhatkhande's *Lakshya Sangitham* of the 20th century; and while on its practical side, it had been raised to the highest pinnacle of glory by Tansen in North India and Thiagaraja in South India; the statement of the French Missionary, quoted above, must be deemed to be as bold and unabashed as if we were to say that England, in spite of her Labour Success (nay, Labour Cabinet) and Protestantism, is to-day as uncivilised as she had been, when her body was enslaved by the barons and her soul by the clergymen.

My chief aim in writing this book is to show how the dharmic life of Thiagaraja served to point a moral or adorn a tale; to sketch the various phases of his musical progress and point out how they were connected with the development of his religious and ethical notions; to inquire into the state of music prior to his time and find out whether and, if so, how far he improved it; to show how he consolidated the whole of Madras in the 19th century, much in the same manner as Dr. Rabindranath Tagore does the whole of India (may I say of the World?) in the 20th century; and also to enable the followers of Abbe Dubois to realise that Thiagaraja so successfully developed the *melodic* system of Indian Music as to prove to the world at large that, amidst other things, Indian Music is like the night—pure, deep and tender: while European Music is, like the day, a flowing concourse of vast harmony, composed of concord and discord and many disconnected fragments; that the contrariety of their spirits cannot be helped; for, at the root, Nature itself is divided into day and night; and to complain there is no harmony in Indian Music is tantamount to complaining that there is no Sun in the night; that each system has a beauty of its own, just as day and night have each its own ; that both the systems must be kept and studied apart, without any idea of their fusion ; for, experts have recognised that, from the point of language and climate, Indian Music is destined to be metrical rather than rhythmical, vocal rather than instrumental, individual rather than concerted, and (what is important ?) melodic rather than harmonic ; and that therefore to glorify the one and vilify the other must be attributed to ignorance or arrogance.

Since the genius of India, till recently, revolted against History and left it, as it thought, to low ambition and the pride of kings ; I am constrained to seek, for my *Life of Thiagaraja*, the help of traditions and anecdotes which I hasten to faithfully record here, just as they were faithfully handed on to me, by disciples of Thiagaraja in the direct line, as well as by those who had the rare privilege of actually seeing the gifted musician of Thiruvaiyar, lest otherwise those traditions and anecdotes should, by a further passage of time, lose the ring of genuineness they now possess. I need hardly remind my reader that even "traditions and anecdotes" have a value of their own. "They carry" observed Thackeray "a greater amount of truth in solution than the volume which purports to be all true. Indeed from out of them, we get the expression of the life of the time (which they relate), of the manners, of the movement, the dress, the pleasures, the laughter and the ridicules of society. Can the heaviest historian do more ?"

The first source of my information about Thiagaraja was a Tamil Pundit whom I casually met at Poonamalle in 1895, when I paid there a holiday visit and was the guest of my good maternal uncle, Mr. S. Krishnaswami Aiyar, District Munsif of Poonamalle. The Tamil Pundit was a native of Kovoor, near Poonamalle, for three or four generations. He related to me, amidst other things, all about the interview between Thiagaraja and Sundaresa Mudaliar, just as he had got it from those actually present at that interview.

Early in 1896, I had to remain, for a time, at Thiruvaiyar, where my father, Mr. M. Subbier, was District Munsif; and I availed myself of that opportunity to sit at the feet of Patnam Subramanier and learn from him very many of Thiagaraja's and his own Krithis, not excluding his impressions of Thiagaraja's life. Maha Vythinathier had then been dead; and I was able to meet only his brother, Ramaswamier, the author of the well-known *Peria Purana Kirthanas*, who also contributed to the stock of my knowledge about Thiagaraja.

In 1903-4, I was at Trivandrum, prosecuting my Law studies. There I made the acquaintance, which soon ripened into friendship, of Mr. T. Vedadrisadasa Mudaliar, an Ex-Judge of the Travancore High Court. He was then 80, in the enjoyment of sound health. He and his father, Mr. Sulochana Mudaliar (the builder of the Tinnevelly Bridge) had been to Thiruvaiyar and seen Thiagaraja with their own eyes. It was in 1843, five years—as I was told—after the grand historic meeting of Thiagaraja and Govinda Marar. Nalla Thambi Mudaliar, who accompanied Marar, was Vedadrisadasa Mudaliar's paternal uncle. I could not see the uncle ; but the nephew Mudaliar told me, in addition to his own impression of the musician, all he had heard from his uncle, regarding the famous meeting. Some particular portions of the conversation, Mr. Vedadrisadasa Mudaliar and myself had, are very important and will be found recorded elsewhere.

Another source was the late Narasimha Bhagavathar who, while at Madras, gave me a mine of information about Thiagaraja, whose works he was then, that is in 1908, editing for the first time in a systematic form.

Still another source was Walajapet to which place I had been, in 1910, to learn Thiagaraja's Krithis as well as some details of his life. I got all that was available there.

I had also the advantage of going through two interesting sketches of Thiagaraja—one by Mr. C. Thirumalayya Naidu and the other by Mr. T. Lakshmana Pillay ; as well as through *Sangitha Sampradaya Pradarsani* (which contains a short memoir of Thiagaraja) of Mr. B. Subbarama Dikshithar ; *Travancore State Manual* Vol. III of 1906 (which contains a cursory account of Thiagaraja) of Mr. V. Nagamayya ; *Dakshinathya Sangitham* (which contains a fragmentary account of Thiagaraja) of Mr. C. R. Srinivasa Aiyangar ; *Thiagaraja Hridayam* (which contains a discursive account of Thiagaraja) of Mr. K. V. Srinivasa Aiyangar ; and also *Thiagaraja Charithram* (which looks like a historical novel) of Mr. Panju Bhagavathar of Thiruvaithanam.

Other sources, too numerous to mention, stood me also in great stead.

The large number of these sources has the same merit and demerit of a large number of witnesses in a court of law. They at once enlighten and confound the truth-seeker. I shall however enter the dim region of Thiagaraja's Life, try to fix beaconlights from place to place and enable any future adventurer to make deeper explorations. But which beaconlight will show me the right path but the emancipated soul of my beloved daughter,

Lakshmi Bai

who was born at Bangalore on November 30, 1911 and died at Dharmapuri on September 10, 1919; and who, just three months prior to the shuffling of her mortal coil, electrified an enlightened audience of Madras with Thiagaraja's *Thelīsi Rama* and elicited therefrom a well-merited applause for the first (alas! the last) time of her life? Yes: my daughter, like the Polar Star, will guide my lonely way: and it is her clarion voice of 'Excelsior' that encourages me to try the Pass, though—

> " Dark lowers the tempest overhead,
> The roaring torrent is deep and wide."

CHAPTER II.

THIAGARAJA'S EARLY LIFE AND EDUCATION.

SRI Thiagaraja's life, like Dr. Tagore's, does not abound with adventures. The fame of both the personages was acquired, alike, in solitude. Any detailed account of their actions would be dry and scarcely distinguish them from the rest of mankind. But the world regards them with love and veneration, because when they came out of their cells, one gave it his unrivalled *Gitanjali*, and the other his unparalleled *Krithis*.

Krithis, in South India, are nowadays the mainstay of a musical performance. You may dispense with Varnas and their paraphernalia; you may dispense with Padas, Javalis, Thillanas, Themmangus, Thiruppuhals, and other kinds of songs which, by sufferance only, dare to peep in at the fag-end of the performance; you may dispense even with Alapana, Pallavi, and Swaras. But dispense with Krithis you cannot; inasmuch as they form the keystone of the concert, while all other species of singing (except perhaps *Pallavi*) are so many minor stones playing only a subordinate part. On a further consideration, it will appear that even 'Pallavi' is essentially a part of Krithi-singing, for it is nothing but an elaboration of the Pallavi-portion of a Krithi. Hence it is right and natural for us to tarry a little and strive to get a glimpse of the crystal source of Krithis, our Thiagaraja; for more than a glimpse we cannot get.

Giriraja Brahmam,* a learned Muriginadu Thrailingya Telugu Brahmin of Bharadwaja Gothra, was our musician's grand father. He was a native of Thiruvalur, now a Junction of South Indian, and Tanjore District Board, Railways, 15 miles to the west of Negapatam. He was well-versed in Sanskrit and Telugu and a good musician to boot. His vedantic songs were appreciated even by the then Raja of Tanjore, Sahaji, who patronised him well. He had five sons, the last of whom was Rama Brahmam.

---

* Giriraja Brahmam was duly immortalised by Thiagaraja in his Bangala Krithi. *Girirajasutha*, though in an indirect way. Some are of opinion that Giriraja was our hero's *maternal* grandfather. But if, as I am told, "Brahmam" was a family title; the inference would become strong that he was Thiagaraja's paternal, rather than maternal, grandfather.

This Rama Brahmam had an innocent wife, Shantha by name, who bore him two sons—Panchanada Brahmam and Thiagaraja Brahmam, our hero.* The following tree illustrates the pedigree of Thiagaraja's family :—

Giriraja Brahmam
|
Rama Brahmam (5th son)
|

Panchanada Brahmam
|
Pattabhirama Brahmam
|
Panchanada Brahmam
|
Pattabhirama Brahmam
alias
Ramudu Aiyar (*living*)

THIAGARAJA
Brahmam
|
Sitalakshmi
|
Thiagaraja

(*Line Extinct*)

Rama Brahmam, our hero's father, adopted the Bhagavathar's † profession and eked out thereby a fair livelihood.

He regarded himself as the legate of the skies, his theme divine, his office sacred, and his credentials clear ; and he delighted to think that he had

* In a Bilahari Krithi, *Thoraguna*, mention is made of Thiagaraja as being the son of Rama Brahmam.

† Bhagavathar means Religious Preacher.

the rare privilege of being a negotiator between God and Man. He might well be proud of his (Bhagavathar's) profession. For, if the whole of humanity be regarded as a big army marching towards the goal of salvation ; Bhagavathars may be said to lead the van, while Judges of Law Courts may be said to bring up the rear. While the functions of both are, alike, to lead man to the right tract ; Bhaghavathars can perform them with greater success than Judges. Murderers may be hanged ; but murder will never cease. If however positive maxims of advice are timely advanced by the preachers, O ! how many crimes will disappear from the world ! Indeed the Bhagavathars' mission is noble, and their function is sacred ; they establish the strong, restore the weak, reclaim the wanderer, and bind the broken heart.

By an irony of fate, the first son of this model man (Rama Brahmam) was from his tender years mature in dulness and stood throughout confirmed in full stupidity. He claimed fraternity with Shadwell and would never deviate into sense ; nor would he allow his genuine night to be mixed with any alloy of light. But his second son, Thiagaraja was :—

"An awful, reverend and religious man;
His eyes diffused a venerable grace,
And charity itself was in his face.
He drew his audience upwards to the sky
And oft with holy songs he charmed their ears
A music more melodious than the spheres."

The cobra of poverty, which Rama Brahmam nurtured, while it retained the purifying gem on its own head, gave out, even on the slightest irritation, the poison of envy, jealousy, and other kindred passions. The younger son took the gem, while the elder the poison.

Thiagaraja, like his contemporary Muthuswami Dikshithar, was born at Thiruvalur, a sacred place noted, from time immemorial, for a Siva temple. Tradition has it that once Indra went to Vishnu and asked him for help against the Rakshasas. Vishnu granted him an image of a God, called Thiagaraja, which acted as a talisman and gave him victory with a warning that he should not, under any circumstances, part with it. In a subsequent fight with another batch of Rakshasas, he sought the help of the King of Thiruvalur, Muchukunda by name, and forgetfully handed over to him the image by way of consideration. Muchukunda defeated the Rakshasas, built a temple at Thiruvalur and established the image of Thiagaraja there. But Indra fell down and was born a Pariah as a matter of punishment. Even to-day a Pariah is permitted at Thiruvalur to precede, as a matter of right, the procession on all festival days, holding a white umbrella, one of the symbols of Indra, from whom he claims to be descended.

While four or five years old, the boy, Thiagaraja, placed under the ferule of a pial School Master—the same ferule as his elder brother had enough suffered from. Every morning therefore he would go to the school as a murderer to the place of execution ; and every evening he would run back with the unbounded hilarity of an escaped convict. A miserable thatched building in a dirty lane ; a heart-rending scene of half-famished children groaning under the lashes of their dwarfish teacher ; the reddening of his eyes if some of his pet boys failed to furnish him daily with snuff and on festive occasions with cakes ; the hasty and the breakneck speed of teaching lessons, if the teacher had to run to a neighbouring village to receive his *dakshina* at a funeral ceremony ; the slipshod and half-sleeping way of hearing the boys repeat their old lessons, whenever there was no call from outside ; the curious custom of caning the boys even when they behaved well, on the still more curious ground that they must often be put in mind of what they would receive, if they might err ; the wretched cudgan leaves to read ; the chilling sand to write ; and the iron thorn to prick from below, if a delinquent boy (probably a snuff or cake defaulter) happened to slip down, while hanging with his hands tied to a beam above ; these were the early surroundings which the infant Thiagaraja had to face.

The fear of his first son's going astray necessitated Rama Brahmam to shift to Thiruvaiyar, bag and baggage, and give at least his second son the benefit of College education available there. So, within a year of Thiagaraja's educational career, the father migrated along with his family from Thiruvalur to Thiruvaiyar—a place noted for a Sanskrit College and salubrious climate and situated on the left bank of the Cauvery, about 6 miles to the north of Tanjore.

Thiruvaiyar, rendered more holy by its association with Thiagaraja's name, had been, all along, itself a holy place of pilgrimage. It is regarded as the Punjab of South India. Why, its sanskrit name is Panchanada, for five rivers, viz. the Coleroon, the Cauvery, the Kodamuruti, the Vettar, and the Vennar—all run in nearly parallel courses within a distance of six miles from it. The sanctity of the town is so great that there is a saying :

காசிக்கு வீசம் அதிகம் திருவையாறு.

(*Thiruvaiyar is holier than Benares by one-sixteenth*)

Once a Brahmin, who was going to Benares to throw his father's bones into the Ganjes, halted a night at Thiruvaiyar on the way. When he awoke in the morning, he found that the bones had assumed the shape of a *Linga*, Siva's emblem. He at once deposited them in the Cauvery and stopped his journey to Benares. Many aged Brahmins thenceforward resorted to Thiruvaiyar in the hope of dying there. That it is blessed to die there is explained by a legend of a boy who was killed by Yama, the God of Death, while worshipping the God of five rivers. The latter God, Panchanadisa, thereupon killed Yama but restored him to life on condition that he should not molest those who died at Thiruvaiyar or within sight of the smoke of the incense burnt at the temple there. In a great pit, in front of the southern gate of the temple, incense is continually burnt to the God Alkondar and a statue of the deity represents him as a collosal figure crushing Yama under his feet.

Again, the temple of Thiruvaiyar is the chief of seven neighbouring shrines, called Saptha-sthanam, all within three miles' radius of Thiruvaiyar: the legend says that the bull Nandi was married under the auspices of the God at Thirumalavedi and taken in procession round these seven places ending with Thiruvaiyar. The Blue Books describe the place as a seat of Sanskrit Learning and also as the sanatorium of the Rajas of Tanjore. The two modern celebrities, Maha Vythinathier (1852 to 1893) and Patnam Subramanier, (1845 to 1902) lived there quite recently.

To this holy place it was that our future musician was brought even during his infancy; and in this new place of settlement, Rama Brahmam experienced no difficulty in establishing his name as a first-rate Bhagavathar. Yet, he felt himself unhappy: for, the same pial-school as he wanted to avoid in Thiruvalur stared him in the face even at Thiruvaiyar. Lo! the same kind of teacher was there with—

"The indented stick that lost day by day,

Notch after notch, till all were smoothed away."

Teaching was only one of his many-sided activities; for, he was at once a money-lender, astrologer, purohith, and cardsplayer. Yet by himself or proxy, he successfully kept all his boys throughout the day from mischief at home; and that was all the parents wanted.

The innate shrewdness of Rama Brahmam, with a painful memory of a former failure, now whipped him to take up himself the work of 'First Aid' in education to his dear Thiagaraja. He therefore taught him the 3 R's and soon initiated him into the high principles of morality more by his own example than by precept. For, he learnt by bitter experience, consequent upon the ruin of his first, school-exposed boy, that the most telling way of teaching moral principles was to make them felt betimes in the midst of a well-regulated family where the child, seeing them put into actual practice every day, would form moral habits, so that when he reached years of responsibility, those habits would be already ingrained in him to such an extent as to incapicitate him to fall a prey to any kind of temptation whatsoever; and his conscience would have no need to argue but would cry aloud against the temptation with the revolt of invincible disgust.

After five years of home-education, the father proceeded to get his boy admitted into the Sanskrit

College of Thiruvaiyar. But the mother, Shantha, insisted that her dear Thiagu (for, so Shantha called Thiagaraja) should be brought up in the family profession of Bhagavathar. Thus with regard to the future of Thiagaraja, his parents happened to take different views ; and their further conversation showed that the mother alone, more than the father, had the instinct to foresee the son's future greatness.

Rama Brahmam :—Why should I not break the tradition and train our boy for a teachership in the College ?

Shantha:—A teachership in the College ! No, my dear Thiagu should be, like Purandara Das of old, a teacher of our Country.

Rama Brahmam :—But Purandara Das was a rich man and a gem-merchant too. He could afford to travel from Pandrapur to Rameswaram and from Rameswaram to Udipi and leave, behind, the stamp of his Githas and Kirthanas, which the people received along with the money he presented.

Shantha :—I don't know all that. A few months back, I happened to teach Thiagu a few Kirthanas, some from Purandara Das and some from

Rama Das, which I had learnt from my father. To my surprise, I found he had such a nice voice as to make me think that he might, if God willed, eclipse both the Dases.

Rama Brahmam :—This is too early an estimate. Ever since my bubble-castle about Jyappesan (for, so Panchanada was called by his parents) was blown-up, I learnt a bitter lesson that boys were, at best, but pretty buds unblown, the scent and hues whereof could only be guessed but unknown.

Shantha :—True ; but the blowing-up of your bubble-castle was due to your mistake, to which I confess I was an abettor, of applying yourself to Jyappesan's own disposition which, when unfurled, showed—like the sail of the boat whereby we went to Rameswaram—all its rents and patches to us. Generally speaking, parents in their first inexperience commit the same mistake with regard to their first-born son. A younger son, like a second wife, is commonly fortunate. Pray, let us avoid our first mistake and bring up our Thiagu, according to our own disposition.

Rama Brahmam :—What objection have you to get our boy admitted into the College ?

Shantha :—What nourishment is there to feed Thiagu's growing mind but verbs conjugated and nouns declined ?

Rama Brahmam :—O ! that's inevitable. Myself passed through that stage. But in this College there is a happy diversion, namely, the teaching of Puranas and Ithihasas in the Vernacular, side by side with Sanskrit teaching.

Shantha :—Then, let our boy go. But in the heart of my hearts I would see him rather a pleasing musician than a boring teacher. Something in my mind tells me that he will, ere long, be, what I wish him to be.

The College, which Thiagaraja now joined, was—I am told—founded by Govinda Dikshithar, Prime-Minister of Achyuthappa Naick, at the end of the 16th century. With a high ambition of having all the ancient Universities rolled into this College, the Prime-Minister introduced, into his Institution, the Medicine of Taxila, the Logic of Nalanda, the Astronomy of Ujjain, the Tanthra of Vikramasila, the Dramatic Literature of Kanouj, and the Vedantic Literature of Benares. He even wanted to make due provisions for vocational instruction and fine arts ; but his life was cut away. In the hands of his successors, the College began to mark time ; and, when the Nawab of Arcot interfered with the affairs of Tanjore, it came to be uncared-for and degenerated into a factory of literary drudges. At the time, however, when our Thiagaraja joined the College, the tone of the Institution was a little improved and the subject of instruction comprised the two Epics and Bhagavatham in Vernacular and Vyakaranam, Logic and Vedas in Sanskrit.

Within four years of his College career, the young boy managed to master, amidst other matters, the contents of the *Ramayana*, for which he somehow formed a special attachment. If a truant class-mate tempted him to take French leave for a day and go in for a dog-chase, he would reply ; "I am already engaged in accompanying my Rama in his chase after the golden deer." If a desperate bully advised him to create a scene of lock-out in the College, he would retort : "Has there been a more cross and peevish teacher than Viswamithra ? And what a docile and obedient student he had in my dear Rama ?" And if his brother's courtezan went, whether of her own accord or under inducement, to mislead the budding musician, he would forthwith tell her : "Do you remember what became of Surpanaka, when she teased Rama in season and out of season ?"

Thus when his friends and fellow students were, in addition to various forms of mischief, stuffing their memory with the Aorist form of third conjugation roots and other substitutes for true knowledge; Thiagaraja was familiarising himself with every detail of the long story of Sri Rama and laying, unknowingly though, a strong foundation for the subject-matter of his remarkable krithis, yet to be composed.

CHAPTER III.

HIS DATE.

THE date of Thiagaraja's birth is not so accurately handed on to us as that of his death. Mr. Panju Bhagavathar wrote, in his *Thiagaraja Charithram*,[1] what he had learnt from his guru, Ramiengar, one of the direct pupils of Thiagaraja's; "Thiagaraja died in 4948th year of Kali Yuga, Parabhava, Pushya Bahula Panchami." Messrs. Narasimha Bhagavathar[2], Ramananda Yogi,[3] Adi and Co.,[4] K.V. Srinivasa Aiyangar,[5] P.V. Krishnaswamier, B.A., B.L.,[6] and Nagaraja Bhagavathar[7]

1 Vide its Edition of 1917—page 52.

2 Vide the Introduction to his Edition (1908) of Thiagaraja's Works p. 16.

3 „ „ (1910) „ „ p. 11.

4 their „ (1916) „ „ p. 12.

5 Vide the Introduction to his Re-Edition (1921) of Ramanand Yogi's Thiagaraja's Works—page 30.

6 Vide his Essay on *Thiagaraja*, published in the Fourth Quarterly Report (1913)—page 32 of Tanjore Sangitha Vidya Mahajana Sangam.

7 Vide his Essay on *Thiagaraja*, in the same Report—page 53.

have each referred to the same year as the date of Thiagaraja's death. Further, Thiagaraja's *Aradhana* (that is, Anniversary of his death), that has been regularly taking place year after year, used to be calculated from the self-same date. Hence we may take it for certain that Thiagaraja died in 4948th year of Kali Yuga, Parabhava, Pushya Bahula Paṇchaṃi, according to lunar reckoning; *or* Parabhava Panchami just prior to Thai Amavasya, 24th of Dhanus or Margali, according to solar reckoning; both of which, alike, correspond to Wednesday, January 6, 1847.

But, in his *Thiagaraja Hridayam* * Mr. K. V. Srinivasa Aiyangar, like Mr. E. Clements of Bombay,† wrote: "Thiagaraja died in 1846." His mistake is evidently due to the fact that the Indian Year, Parabhava, corresponded to two English years 1846 and 1847; and that he chose 1846 as the most probable year, without however taking trouble to refer even to an ordinary panchangam. At any rate, he is near the mark. But far away from it, ran Mr. V. Nagamayya, when he stated, in a responsible Government publication,‡ that "Thiagaraja died in 1842"!

---

* Vide its Edition of 1922. Vol. 1, page 8.
† Vide his *Ragas of Tanjore*, page 48..
‡ Vide *Travancore State Manual*—Vol. III (1906)—page 254.

A reference to Mr. Ramudu Aiyar (the only surviving member of Thiagaraja's family) *or* the well-known way of calculating our musician's "*Aradhana-Day*" would have set right the Dewan Peishcar's view. Why, the very person—Mr. T. Lakshmana Pillay—from whom Mr. Nagamayya admittedly* got all his information on music for his *State Manual*, correctly wrote :† "Thiagaraja died a very old man in 1847." Surely, the State Officer was too proud to be imitative, though right ; and preferred to be original, though wrong. Further, his statement (viz., Thiagaraja died in 1842) becomes all the more incredible, in view of the fact (which we shall presently learn) that his neighbour Mr. Vedadrisadasa Mudaliar had an interview with Thiagaraja, next year, that is, in 1843. The right date of Thiagaraja's death is, as mentioned above, 6th of January 1847.

Can we ascertain the date of his birth from the age at which he died ? But, while Captain C. R. Day ‡ gave Thiagaraja only 20 years of

---

* Vide *Travancore State Manual* (Vol. III) (1906.) —page 252. Footnote.

† In his *Essays*—page 140.

‡ In his *South Indian Music*, page 155. Captain Day gives 1820 to 1840 as Thiagaraja's date.

life ; Rev. H. A. Popley[1] gave him only 50 ; Mr. C. Thirumalayya Naidu[2] gave him 75 ; Mr. B. Subbarama Dikshithar,[3] 77 ; Mr. T. Lakshmana Pillay,[4] 80 ; Messrs. V. Nagamayya[5] and K. V. Srinivasa Aiyangar,[6] 82 ; Messrs. Narasimha Bhagavathar,[7] Ramananda Yogi,[8] and Adi and Co.,[9] 88 ; and Mr. C. R. Srinivasa Aiyangar,[10] 89. How are we to get out of this difficulty ?

Weighing, however, the balance of evidence, the testimony of Mr. Narasimha Bhagavathar and

---

1 In his *Music of India* (1921). Mr. H. A. P. gives. as Thiagraja's date 1800 to 1850.—page 22.

2 Vide his *Tyagayyar*—page 8.

3 Vide his *Sangitha Sampradaya Pradarsani* (Life of Musicians) page 24.

4 Vide his *Essays*—page 153.

5 Vide his *State Manual* Vol. III, page 254.

6 In his *Thiagaraja Hridayam*, Mr. K. V. S. gives, as Thiagaraja's date, 1764 to 1846.

7 Vide his Introduction to Thiagaraja's Krithis —page-15.

8 Vide „ „ „ „ —page-10.

9 Vide „ „ „ „ —page-11.

10 In his *Dakshinaihya Sangitham* Mr. C. R. S. writes that Thiagaraja was 15 when his mother died in 1773.

his followers is entitled to our credit; as it at once gets itself corroborated by that of Mr. Panju Bhagavathar who, be it remembered, was a pupil of a direct pupil of Thiagaraja's and who alone, of all our musician's biographers, ventured under a right inspiration to record: "Thiagaraja was born in 4859th year of Kali Yuga, Bahudanya."*

Now, Bahudanya to Bahudanya gives us 60 years; and Bahudanya to Parabhava gives us 28 years. In all, therefore, Thiagaraja lived, according to Mr. Panju Bhagavathar, for (60+28=) 88 years. To the same 88 years the result of my own investigation points. I said that there were some important portions of my conversation with Mr. T. Vedadrisadasa Mudaliar which I should like to have recorded here. Here is one of them:—

Myself:—In what year did you meet Thiagaraja?

Mudaliar:—1843.

Myself:—How old was he then?

Mudaliar:—He was then as old as I now am, perhaps a little older. He must be 84; for, I remember my uncle having told me that he

---

* Vide his *Thiagaraja Charithram*, page 9.

had heard Thiagaraja giving his own age to be 79 in 1838*.

If Thiagaraja was, according to Mr. Vedadrisadasa Mudaliar 84 in 1843; *or* according to himself, 79 in 1838; the date of his birth must, by mere arithmetical calculation, be 1759.† We may now safely state that our great musician-saint lived in this world, for 88 years, from 1759 to 1847.

---

* That Thiagaraja and Govinda Marar met in 1838 and that Mr. Vedadrisadasa Mudaliar saw Thiagaraja with his own eyes at Thiruvaiyar in 1843—are both confirmed by Mr. T. Lashmana Pillay, whose source of information seems to be the same as mine. As to how Thiagaraja gave his own age to be 79 in 1838, see below.

† Mr. K. V. Srinivasa Aiyangar's date of Thiagaraja's birth (viz. 1764) is obviously wrong.

CHAPTER IV.

HIS INITIATION INTO MUSIC.

THIAGARAJA'S initiation into music, for which he is now more remembered, came about, as it were by chance, as seems to be the case with most great men. England, for instance, would not have been able to boast of a heaven-born General and Founder of the British Empire in India, if Richard Clive had not shipped off his son, Robert, to make a fortune or to die of fever, at Madras. Scotland would not have been able to boast of a prolific Novelist, if Lord Byron had not driven Sir Walter Scott from the field of poetry. Germany would not have been able to boast of the author of *Messiah*, if the Duke of Saxe-Weissenfels had not persuaded the elder Handel to transfer his son, Handel, from Law to music. India would not have been able to boast of the author of *Sakunthala*, if the disappointed suitors had not revengefully conspired to dupe the learned but haughty Princess Vidyakrosa into marrying a veritable dunce of Kalidasa. Similarly we would not have been able to boast of the author of *Krithis*, if Sonti Venkatramanayya had not allured Thiagaraja from Literature to Music.

In North Street of Thiruvaiyar, there happened to live a Vynika, named Venkatramana Das *alias* Sonti Venkatramanayya [1] son of Sonti Venkatasubbayya, under whom many a pupil was learning music. To listen to this Palace-Vidwan's songs, our little boy would steal an hour or two from the rigid time-table imposed on him both at home and in the College. Such, however, was the love he acquired for the Art and such was the warmth he felt for its pleasures that he contracted a positive hatred for the Logic of Tharka[2] and the dreary subtleties of Vyakarana, wherewith his College atmosphere was surcharged.

In this respect, he resembled Voltaire of France. Both of them neglected severe studies and loved pleasurable arts. The punishments of the Academy and the exhortations of their elders were; alike, insufficient to influence them. Anything that wore the face of industry they carefully avoided ; and whereever pleasure presented, they were foremost in the pursuit. In conducting these

1. His house is still to be seen in the North Street.

2. Note Thiagaraja's Query : *Vada Tharkamu Ela* in his Kalyani Krithi " Bhajana Sayave Manasa."

two boys of so refractory a disposition, any one else would have redoubled his punishment or discontinued his care. But Poree in the case of Voltaire and Rama Brahmam in the case of Thiagaraja perceived that all their attempts to thwart nature were of no avail ; and they resolved to indulge the genius of their respective boys in their own favourite pursuits, literature and music, respectively.

Soon did Thiagaraja leave his *Alma Mater* with the character of an old unaccountable fellow that had a great deal of learning. Quite instinctively did he decide to dedicate his whole life to Music, not as a means but as an end in itself, not as a recreation but as a serious life-work.* For, as Ruskin rightly observed, " Art, properly so-called, is no recreation ; it cannot be learnt at spare moments, nor pursued when we have nothing better to do ; it is no handiwork for the drawing-room, no relief of the ennui of boudoirs; it must be understood and undertaken seriously or not at all."

Rama Brahmam heartily congratulated his wife on the fulfilment of her prophesy and most willingly introduced his self-willed boy to the Palace-Vidwan, Sonti Venkatramanayya. The guru soon found that his new pupil had already

*Cf. His Asaveri Krithi " Eh Paniko."

with him a good stock of Kirthanas of both the Dases and proceeded to work upon those materials. In other words, he polished those Krithanas and taught them again to the boy on up-to-date lines. Thiagaraja learnt thus to sing in a sweet voice many a devotional song. When Patnam Subramanier queried in his own krithi, *Dhanyudevvado*: "Who indeed is the blessed person that worships you, O! Dasarathi! with the sweetest music based upon pure and unalloyed swaras and accompanied by superior maddala, thala, thambura, vina and murali?"; he had evidently Thiagaraja in his mind. It seems that our musician sat at the feet of one more guru who taught him the *science* of Music, as contained in a treatise called *Swararnavam.* Tradition says that this guru was Narada himself who, in the guise of a sanyasi, met Thiagaraja, heard him sing and was so pleased that he taught him Tharakamanthra, presented him with 'Swararnavam' and initiated him into the mysteries thereof. The matchless Krithi, *Swararagasudharasa,* forms a fitting acknowledgment of Thiagaraja's indebtedness to 'Swararnavam' and his *Varanarada* in Vijayasri, a happy expression of his gratitude to Narada.

'Swararnavam' seems to have been a very ancient treatise on Indian Music; for Thiagaraja refers to its contents as having been taught to Parvathi by Parameswara. It is a pity that the treatise has been lost to us. Could it have been thrown into the flood of the Cauvery along with Rama's Idol, of which we shall hear later on ? If so, Panchanada Brahmam should have been worse than Newton's dog; for, the latter, unlike the former, could not realise the consequence of its mischief. All that we, therefore, can know of the book, now, is that—even as its name indicates—it dealt with Swaras, their nature, their forms, their varieties and their prastharas. Thiagaraja assures us he has mastered the book and asks us to tread in his wake, with unremitting faith in the efficacy of Swara-learning.

We are glad to see that Thiagaraja anticipated the two burning questions, viz :—

(1) Is Swara-Learning after all necessary ?

(2) Can it not be altogether avoided ?

—questions that have of late been causing much anxiety in South India, in as much as they have emanated from high quarters and attempted to shake the very foundation of Indian Music. We are further glad to note that our musician answered the first question in the affirmative and the second question in the negative.

T. H. denotes Thiagaraja's House.

CHAPTER V.

HIS BATTLE OF LIFE.

THE period of education over, Thiagaraja lost his parents and his ancestral property was partitioned between himself and his aggressive brother. To his share, fell only a small house[1] in Thirumanjana Street of Thiruvaiyar and a very fascinating gold image[2] of Sri Rama, which he cherished as the heirloom of his family. Sometime after, the jealous brother, Panchanada, threw Thigaraja's idol into the full-flooded Cauvery. This unfortunate incident wrang from our devotee a typical Thodi Krithi, *Endudakinado* : " Where has Rama concealed himself and when would he show me mercy and come back here ? When long ago the firm-minded Prahlada was treated with great brutality by his father,

1. That, on partition, a house fell to the lot of Thiagaraja wherewith he was satisfied ; that his aggressive brother and his party used to accuse him of false charges ; and that he did not allow his mind to be affected by these taunts—these things are all set forth in his Madhyamavathi song, *Nadupai palikeru.*

2. This self-same gold image is now with Subramani Josier, Varahappier's Lane, South Main Street, Tanjore.

Hiranyakasipu ; did not my God first conceal himself in a pillar and then come out of it to help his Bhaktha ? When again Vali, Indra's son, mercilessly thrashed his brother, Sugriva ; did not my God first conceal himself in the branches of a tree and then kill the aggressor ? Now too, that he may crush my six enemies,[1] he has no doubt concealed himself ; but where ?" To search for the idol he began ; and his Harikamboji song, *Nenenduvedakudura*, "Where shall I search for you ?" indicates the depth of his grief ; and the broken way in which words are set therein is proof thereof. When he subsequently discovered his idol, he was all ecstasy ; and profuse songs in praise of Rama poured forth from his full heart. He took the idol in procession around the town and sang, in particular, two improvised songs, viz., *Etladorakithivo* and *Sallare*, meaning respectively "How I got you back ?" and "Shower flowers on Rama."

But what did Thiagaraja do to make a living ? The problem of keeping the wolf off the door was like a false note in a sweet song which he would not listen to, nor could he endure it. For, he had

1. The six enemies are :—Kama, Krodha, Lobha, Moha, Mada and Mathsarya.

ever been of opinion that the Law of the Universe was nothing else then the Law of his own Body, writ large. Does not the stomach digest for digestion's sake? Do not the lungs respire for respiration's sake? If the stomach refuses to sacrifice its all and to live on whatever share of its sacrifice comes back to it, but keeps undigested a portion of what it gets to itself; or if the lungs think it beneath their dignity to do their scavenging work and thus keep their oxygen to themselves; the (physio-) logical result will be purging, vomiting or suffocation, as the case may be. Hence the various limbs of the body perform their respective functions and sacrifice their all, for sacrifice' sake, and get back, as a matter of course, the Yangya Sishta [1] or the remains of sacrifice, whereby the common economy of the body is preserved. Much in the same manner, Thiagaraja, as a limb of the Body Politic, gave out his music to the world as a

---

यज्ञशिष्टाशिनःसंतोमुच्यंतेसर्वाकेल्बिषैः

1. Cf. The righteous, who eat the remains of sacrifice are freed from all sins.—Gita.

4. Dr. Tagore's view on Oonchvrithi ; "When we get our food precariously as alms, we remember God, the giver. But when we receive our food regularly at home, as a matter of course, we are apt to regard it as ours by right" —*The Devotee.* Swami Vivekananda observed in this connection:—"India will be raised, not by the power of wealth but of the *begging* bowl."

matter of sacrifice and got, as a matter of course, his own 'Yangya Sishta' in the shape of '*Oonchorithi*' rice. He would one day emerge from his cottage; go along the principal streets of Thiruvaiyar with his disciples all singing; draw, as he marched, an ever-increasing throng of pious admirers behind; collect rice, *given copiously and willingly*, sufficient to maintain him, his family, and his disciples for about a week; and then retreat, till the next necessity arose, into his cell, where he divided his time between praying, preaching, composing, and teaching and where even rogues that went to scoff remained to pray and listened.

Knowing full well that—

> "Alas! the joys that fortune brings
> Are trifling and decay;
> And those who prize the paltry things
> More trifling still than they;"

our saintly musician deliberately forewent all wordly pleasures; chose, with superior courage, to lead a simple and unpretentious life; and enjoyed all the blessings of poverty, such as even kings might descend from their thrones only to slumber undisturbed in its elysium.

---

1. cf. ஏற்பதிகழ்ச்சி—

It is mean to beg—Auvai.

The fashionable world may sneer at Thiagaraja, because he chose to be a mendicant; and may deem him to be insensible, because he did not feel the ignominy[1] of receving. But, as Mr. Laskshmana Pillay powerfully retorts, which profession is wholly exempt from dependence upon the people? Do you believe that passing money at a counter, or distributing salt, or drafting a number of letters at an office desk, or even skilfully pleading a bad case, are the only ways of serving the people? No, no. How much did Thiagaraja's songs help to soothe, elevate, and inspire the people of his time and even after? What nobler service can any man do to the world than he and what, in comparison with it, was the return he looked for? The "oonchvrithi rice" given to him was, be it remembered, wages of merit, which he could rightly demand, and not unmerited bounty granted to him by impulsive generosity. By "the ignominy of receiving," Altangi, who used the phrase, referred only to extorted benevolence and not to the natural, and even polticial, subordination which subsists in every society where the obligation is mutual on either side,

---

1 cf. வம்மின் புலவீர்! நும்மெய் வருந்திக்கைசெய்து உய்மினோ' (Welcome Poets ! Earn your livelihood by the sweat of your brow).

Moreover, our musician was a firm believer in Nammalwar's dictum and thought, along with him, that learning had nothing to do with earning, in as much as the former had for its object the development of the soul and the latter only the upkeep of the body; and that whoever transgressed the dictum and attempted to earn by learning must, subject to freakish exceptions, necessarily undergo a servere suffering here. How far Nammalwar and Thiagaraja were right in their views may easily be estimated by surveying the general lot of such transgressing artists all over the world, whether of poetry, painting, or music.

In Greece, Homer's mouth was more frequently filled with verses than with bread. In Italy, Tasso begged the light of his cat's eyes to write by, being too poor to afford himself a candle. In Spain, the great Cervantes died of hunger. In France, Vaugleas got the notorious title of the Owl, because he kept himself within doors all day and ventured to come out of them only by night, for fear of his creditors. In England, staggering under a load of debt and labour, tracked by bailiffs and reproachful creditors, devising fevered plans for the morrow, at last, at five and forty, death seized poor Oliver Goldsmith and closed his career.

As for the lot of painters, the life of Caravagio of Rome was a convincing example to show that his fraternity flourished, like medical plants, in a region of savageness and barbarity, their excellence unknown and their virtues unheeded. Poor Caravagio's name went very high, just when at nightfall, he was found dead by the road side, overcome by fatigue, resentment, and despair.

Take the case of Musicians. Mozart was frequently obliged to pawn his gifts to purchase a dinner and lodging. "What a comment on the period," wrote Ferris, "which adored genius but allowed it to starve! His audience could be enthusiastic enough to carry him to his hotel on their shoulders but probably never thought that the wherewithal of a hearty supper was a more seasonable homage".

Turn we now to India. Kabir and Thiruvalluvar had, for their living, to weave cloth along with their immortal works. Auvai had to sing for salt and tamarind—

> " உப்புக்கும்பாடி புளிக்குமொரு கவிதை
> ஒப்பிக்குமென்ற னுளம்."[1]

---

1. My mind has stooped even to sing a song for (a handful of) salt and compose a stanza for tamarind.

Padikkasu Thambiran had to confess the wretched predicament into which poets, as a class, had fallen after the Sangam period—

“மூவேந்தருமற்றுச் சங்கமும்போய்ப்
பதின்மூன்றொ டெட்டுக்
கோவேந்தருமற்று மற்றொருவேந்தன்
கொடையுமற்றுப்
பாவேந்தர் காற்றி லிலவம்
பஞ்சாகப் பறந்தனரே.,”[2]

and found fault with himself for using learning for earning :—

“அடகெடுவாய் பலதொழிலு மிருக்கக்கல்வி
அதிகமென்றே கற்றுவிட்டோ மறிவில்லாமல் ;
திடமுள மோகனமாடக் கழைக்கூத்தாடச்
செம்பிடு வித்தைகளாடத் தெரிந்தோமில்லை ;
தடமுலை வேசையராகப் பிறந்தோமில்லைச்
சரியான தமிழைவிட்டுத் தையலார்தம்
இடமிருந்து தூதுசென்று பிழைத்தோமில்லை ;
என்ன ஜன்மமெடுத்துலகி லிரக்கின்றோமே ?”[3]

---

2. The three chief kings are gone ; the Tamil Sangam is gone ; and even the twenty one minor kings are gone. There is thus no king now to encourage poets who therefore hang, like cotton, in the air.

3. Fie upon us, foolish Poets ; While in the world there are very many means of earning, we, in our supine ignorance, attached undue importance to learning and acquired it. What a pitiable life therefore we have been leading ! We regret we have not long ago given up this wretched learning and acquired the art of dancing, performing acrobats or practising jugglery. We also regret we had not been born as swollen breasted concubines or even as pimps for them.

A modern poet whose pitiable condition had driven him only to snuff up the scent of what he could not afford to taste, exclaimed :

> " எண்ணாங்கு முப்பத்திரண்டு பற்காட்டி
>   யிசையுடனே
> பண்ணாகச் செந்தமிழ்
>   பாடிவந்தாலு மிப்பாரிலுள்ளோர்
> அண்ணாந்து பார்ப்பரழகழகென்ப
>   ரதன் பிறகோர்
> சுண்ணாம்புபட்ட இலையுங்கொடார்
>   கவி சொன்னவர்க்கே."[4]

And finally a modern musician, when taunted by a wealthy man with 'காசா லேசா', retorted with an envenomed pun 'காசாலே சா'.[5]

---

4. However excellently a Tamil Poet may sing with all his thirty two teeth exposed; people here may appreciate his song but will never be disposed to help him even with a betel leaf.

5. This is an excellent pun and consists in the re-shuffling of the four letters of the expression, *viz*, கா (Kâ) ; சா(Sâ) ; லே (lê) ; சா (sâ) ; காசு (Kâsu) ; means *money* ; and லேசு (lêsu) means *light*. So when the wealthy man said காசா லேசா (Kâsâ lêsâ) which literally mean "Is money light ? " ; he meant to say 'Is money so light a thing that it can easily be given to you even for your music ? ' The musician's reply, காசாலே சா (Kâsâlê sâ), literally means ' by money, die ; that is, let the money, you seem to make much of, be the very cause of your death.

Very many things similar to these, Thiagaraja knew, some instinctively and some historically too. Hence he courted, instead of being forced into, a life of easy contentment ; refused to expose himself to the weather-like whims of lords and, as we shall see, of even sovereigns ; and found the Public, collectively considered, to be capable of being a good and generous master.

CHAPTER VI.

HIS AGE.

FURTHER, our Thiagaraja, was an excellent reader of his times and felt that, when he came into the world, the age of patronage had passed away.

Time was when music flourished splendidly under the munificent patronage of large-hearted sovereigns who were shrewd enough to understand that the chief component of mind was Feeling more than Intellect; that the former was a master, while the latter a servant; that mere intellectual education was tantamount to educating the servant, while keeping the master a supine ignoramus; and that the nett-result of such an education would be the conversion of the so-called servants into heartless masters, under whose (mis—) guidance society would degenerate into an unnatural institution, enmeshing proud man into an ensnaring habit of vilifying others only to glorify himself and of destroying them only to be himself destroyed. Hence, in Ancient, and even

Medieaval, India, music was held in high esteem, even without any Arcadian pressure. Princes loved it ; princesses practised it ; nobles revelled in it ; and the very people transposted themselves therewith.

But, unfortunately, the age of Thiagaraja, like the age of Samuel Johnson, was a transition period, a period between the age of patronage that had passed away and the age of intelligent public support that had not yet arrived. It was a dark night between two sunny days. As I observed in my *Lectures on Indian Music* : "Not long after the advent of the Europeans, the Goddess of Indian music had to jump from the palace into the open street where—

> "............................ scorn'd and poor,
> She begged her bread from door to door
> And tuned, to please a peasant's ear,
> The harp a king had loved to hear."

A peep into the political condition, during the age of Thiagaraja, of South India in general and of Tanjore in particular will amply bear out my conclusions. Just three years prior to the birth of Thiagaraja, the Seven Year's War broke out in Europe. It was a war mainly between England and France. Hence the English and the French in India warred with each other. Clive destroyed *Dupleix-fatteh-bad* and thereby created a lot of heart-burning which forced the English to further contend against Mysore, the. Karnatic, and Tanjore. The four Mysore Wars impoverished the province and deprived it of Canara, Coimbatore, Wynad, and the Ceded Districts.

And the British Rule over the remaining territory, indirect from 1799 to 1831 and direct from 1831 to 1881, had not, in its programme, the encourgement of music.

As for Tanjore, it went under the British Rule exactly in the year of the fall of Seringapatam. Long before the birth of Thiagaraja, the Nayak Rule had ended and the Maharastra Rule had begun. The confused revolutions during the time of Tukoji's sons were also over. A trembling sovereign, who was ever in the grip of the Nawab of Arcot, sat on the throne of Tanjore in 1773, when the country was subdued and handed over to the Nawab, though, three years hence, it was restored to the Raja. In 1781, Hyder devastated Tanjore ; and in 1787, Saraboji was declared incompetent to rule, though eleven years hence he was again made Raja. In 1799, this Saraboji surrendered his kingdom to the East India Com-

4

pany, having secured for himself a good pension. He and his son Sivaji were the last Rajas of Tanjore and died respectively in 1832 and 1855.

This historical sketch will, it is hoped, convince the reader that the confused state of south India, during the time of Thiagaraja, hampered the growth of the Fine Arts and brought about a paucity of musicians both in Mysore and Tanjore. The only South Indian 'Native State' that escaped from the ravages of war and that enjoyed peace, while, all around, war was going on—was Travancore, even the threatened invasion whereof by Tippu was averted by the timely fall of Seringapatam in 1799. Consequently music flourished there. The musicians of Mysore and Tanjore, after the fall of their kingdoms, slowly moved to the southern-most State and found it safer to live there than elsewhere.

The 'Peace of Travancore' was ensured to them—the *Peace* that had been inaugurated, in 1750, by the able king, Marthanda Varma, who ruled the state from 1729 to 1758 and who, by a bold stroke of policy, dedicated the whole of Travancore, on one fine morning in January 1750, to Sri Padmanabhaswami, for the better safety of his ancient house, and assumed the management of the country as the vassal of the deity and thereby made the people regard Travancore as the possession of God and the person of the Sovereign as His representative. His successor, Rama Varma (1758 to 1798), continued to preserve the peace and order of the country so successfully that he was called "the Father of his people." It was during the reign of this Rama Varma that musicians began to be attracted from far and near by the magnetic personality of the nephew of Marthanda Varma viz. Prince Aswathi who lived from 1756 to 1788 and who was an accomplished Sanskrit scholar and expert musician and whose kirthanas are sung in the temple even to-day. The flow of foreign musicians into the State went on, uninterruptedly, during the reigns of Avittam Thirunal (1798 to 1810) and Gowri Lakshmi Bai (1810 to 1829), till the volume of it grew very large by the special encouragement held out by that musician-sovereign, Swathi Thirumal (1829 to 1847).

Enough, I think, has been said to show that the troublous condition of South India and the peaceful one of Travancore, during the age of Thiagaraja, conspired together to shift the patronage of music from the former to the latter.

CHAPTER VII

HIS SPIRIT.

IT is no wonder, therefore, that two similar transition periods in South India and England produced, in the two countries, two persons of a similar temperament. Both of them found in their respective countries only *fac-simile* patrons who looked with unconcern on men struggling for life n water and, when they reached ground, encumbered them with unnecessary help; and hence both of them looked down upon the so-called patrons with a contempt of the most sovereign character. While, in England, Dr. Johnson exclaimed:

> Deign on the passing world to turn thine eyes
> And pause a while from letters to be wise;
> There mark what ills the scholar's life assail,
> Toil, envy, want, the patron, and the jail;
> See nations, slowly wise and meanly just,
> To buried merit raise the tardy bust.

Thiagaraja in South India sang: *Samayamu-thelisi.* "What is to me whether wealthy men live or die, if they do not by their riches acquire in time *punya* or virtue? What again is it to me whether those men appreciate or depreciate the Arts, who allow themselves to be brought under the category of Lunatics? Inasmuch as the eyes of a person have become blind, what is it to me whether the eyelids remain open or closed? In as much again as the master of a Crore does not pursue the right way, what is it to me whether he becomes a devil or a miser?"

Here the similarity between the two great men stops. For, as soon as George III was pleased to grant Dr. Johnson an annual pension of £300, the Doctor became all respect to His Majesty, would start up and stand still before him, feel himself honored by conversing with him, love to relate to his friends all such conversations with all attendant circumstances and was never tired of praising the manners of the king and declaring them to be as fine as those of Louis XIV or Charles II. When he was once taunted as to how a Jacobite, that he was, could dare to accept a pension from a Hanoverian Sovereign, he replied with a smile: "I wish my pension were twice as large, that my enemies might make twice as much noise. It is true that I cannot now curse the House of Hanover, nor would it be decent for me to drink King James's health in the wine that King George gives me money to pay for. But, Sir, I think that the pleasure of cursing the House of Hanover and drinking King Jame's health. are amply over-balanced by £ 300 a year." As against this mercenary and time-serving Johnson, we shall examine the attitude of our divinely-minded Thiagaraja, when he was twice tempted by seductive Mammon.

Once Saraboji, Raja of Tanjore, sent for Thiagaraja. The messenger met the musician and said: "The Raja offers you a gift of ten *velis* of land and a big bullion of gold, as the price of a song or two, which you are requested to compose in praise of the Raja." The musician replied: "Why should your Raja misuse his wealth in such paltry things as praise and why should I prostitute the Muse's name by flattering kings, many of whom are but plagues and scourges of man-kind, bred up in sloth and ignorance and every vice that nurses both.?" The messenger still persisted and drew Thiagaraja's pointed attention to the bullion of gold. "Fie upon gold," retorted Thiagaraja, "fie upon that cursed gold which ever drives unwary humanity to pursue false joy and suffer real woe. Had I valued gold for its own sake, I should have long ago melted my golden image of Rama into bullion and played, in the twinkling of an eye, drucks and drakes with it. But, to my fortune, my fascinating idol fills my mind with the God inside and not with the gold outside." Then he shot a pointed snatch in Kalyani, *Nidhi Salasukhama*: "Which gives greater joy—wealth or worship in the holy presence of Rama ? O ! Soul ! tell me the truth. Which is sweeter—milk, butter and buttermilk or the essence of the nectar of deep meditation aud bhajana of Dasarathi ! Which conduces more to health—a dip in the Ganjes of firmness and calmness of mind or in the muddy well of depravity? Which of the two is better—praise of haughty man or song on mighty God ? The messenger left without a word more.

On another occasion, H. H. Swathi Thirunal of Travancore sent for Thiagaraja. Vadivelu was the messenger this time. He was one of those musicians who, on the close of the Maharatta Rule at Tanjore, moved to Travancore where he remained long enough to be recognised as the first-rate Violinist of the State. Swathi Thirunal, be it remembered, was himself a great musician and composer. His sister, Rukmini Bai (1809 to 1837) was again a rare poetess and composer of simple yet charming songs, deep yet pure in feelings. Dewan Subba Row too was a musician. Around these principal planets, there moved many a satellite, such as, Govinda Marar, Vadivelu, Sivananda, Chinnayya, Ponnayya, Iravi Varman Thambi, Kshirabdi Sastri, Parameswara Bhagavathar, Meruswami and a host of others. It is no wonder, therefore, that Swathi Thirunal's reign was characterised by one of his successors, Visakam Thirunal, (1880 to 1885) as "the Augustan Age of Travancore Music." While thus Swathi Thirunal was swaying supreme over his peculiar sea of music, a mighty tide from the ocean of Thiagaraja's Krithis splashed on the Maharaja. Kannayya Bhagavathar, a direct disciple of Thiagaraja's, gained an interview with the Maharaja and feasted His Highness's ears with a good set of his guru's *krithis*. Swathi Thirunal was struck dumb with admiration and found that the Travancore Music was to Thiagaraja's what the rancousness of the crow to the song of the nightingale. He yearned to hear Thiagaraja directly and hence commissioned Vadivelu by whatever means to fetch him.

Vadivelu, accordingly, left Trivandrum for Thiruvaiyar. To-day the distance may be covered in less than twenty four hours. But he had to spend many a week and undergo many a privation before he could finish his journey. Even after reaching his destination, he dared not reveal his mission for days together, for he was told of Thiagaraja's previous refusal to Saraboji and feared such another. He waited therefore for a fair opportunity; and at last the inevitable meeting came about. Vadivelu drew a bright picture of Travancore, contrasted it with the stormy condition of Tanjore, touched upon the superior musical qualifications of the Maharaja of Travancore and tried to excite the ambition, if it existed, of Thiagaraja by winding up his message with these words: "For glory's sake come over to Trivandrum." Thiagaraja replied: "What is glory but the people's praise? And who are the people but a confused and miscellaneous rabble that can scarcely distinguish between things sterling, worth the praise and things vulgar, not worth the praise?" Vadivelu changed his line of invitation and said: "Never mind the praise of the rabble. There the Maharaja is eagerly expecting your arrival at Trivandrum. His Highness is sure to raise your *Padavi.*"

"What do you mean by *Padavi*?" interrupted Thiagaraja.

Vadivelu continued: "*Padavi* means High Position. With His Highness as your admiring friend, you will attain full-blown dignity in the State; and the fortune of all, including that of my poor self, will be in your hands. Through your signifying eyes alone, the rays of regal bounty will shine; and at your nod alone, the stream of honor will flow. At your disposal you will have a mountain of wealth which you, your wife and child may enjoy. A high *Padavi* indeed! Do not hesitate to start."

Quite undisturbed in mind, Thiagaraja replied: "You first spoke of glory and now praise riches. I have always regarded wealth to be an impediment to man's progress, quite as much as the baggage would be to that of an army. In either case the march would be hindered and the victory lost or disturbed. Rightly has Lord Krishna said: "Whomsoever I am pleased with, his wealth I take away." Further, excessive wealth makes a man very rarely a donor but very often a miser employing his cares on what he can never enjoy or a prodigal wasting money to purchase what he can never taste. It is thus the toil of fools and the wise man's encumbrance. As for the '*Padavi* you referred to, I have only to draw your attention to my Salakabhairavi Krithi ;—*Padavi Ni Sadbhakthi*' : "That state of mind which places implicit faith in Rama is the real *Padavi*. There are many who have learnt by rote all the Vedas, Shasthras, and Upanishads and can repeat them, parrot-like, from start to finish, but who have not caught their spirit. Can such people be deemed to have attained *Padavi* ? There are many-others who possess a mountain of wealth and a number of wives and children and who enjoy the friendship of Maharajas, Lords of the Earth. Can even they be deemed to have attained *Padavi* ? Again, can a person whose so-called enjoyment is involved in dire ignorance and evil passions, be deemed to have attained *Padavi* ? No, no; only that state of mind which places implicit faith in Rama is the real *Padavi*." Forthwith Vadivelu took leave and went away.

So high-minded was Thiagaraja ; and the world, with all its gold and other attractions, seemed to him either a rock of perils or a vale of tears. He would either pray for emancipation from birth and exclaim with Prior—

"O ! beyond description happiest he,
Who ne'er must roll on life's tumultous sea;
Who, with blessed freedom, from the general doom
Exempt, must never force the teeming womb,
Nor see the Sun, nor sink into the tomb.,"

Or, having been born, would sing along with Lord Krishna—

"He who is able to endure here, ere he be liberated from the body, the impact produced by desire and passion, he is harmonised; he is a happy man."

Here, then, we have a clue as to why Thiagaraja, unlike his English contemporary, refused to be tempted by monetary considerations and why he adopted the *Oonchvrithi* profession that kept him above want and disregarded all greatness as being sterile of solid joys and fertile with trifling toys. Here, again, we understand why, with two warring European nations whose, alternate devastation sapped the resources of all around him; with two sovereigns whose proffered support he spurned with indignation; and with an elder brother whose proffered insult[1] he endured with forbearance ; he had the undaunted courage to shoot above, leaving the sullen earth behind, like a rocket; to

1. Cf. Anadunuganu.

course freely through the silent air; and, having reached the point of culmination, to burst into hundreds of brilliant star-like melodies that would not evaporate and fall but would solidify and crystalize into permanence, much to the wonder of his contemporaries and their successors.

The nearest historical parallel to Thiagaraja was Haridas Swami of Brindavan. These two rare musicians of North and South India—though of different times—were of the same mould and preferred quiet and unostentatious life. They felt no need of human support for their music, because they believed it to be of divine origin. It needed no outside stimulus, proceeded from within and was of manifold variety full of the zeal of faith and love which it inculcated.

CHAPTER VIII.

HIS APPEARANCE AND CHARACTERISTICS.

In appearance, Thiagaraja was a tall lean man of a brown complexion. His shoulders were broad; limbs well proportioned; face stern; forehead broad; larynx fully developed; jaws fleshy but a little pointed at the chin, and chest fairly formed. His flashing eyes were as azure as the heaven; and his noble wife saw heaven nowhere else. The Thulasimala around his neck; the gopinama on his forehead; the chipla in his left hand; the japamala in his right hand, ornamented with a golden ring in the forefinger and a pavithra in the ring finger; the white silk-lined cloth worn with careful folds between and the red silken turban with a broad unfurled tail flowing behind;—all these seem, as it were, to deliver a silent sermon on the efficacy of Plain Living and High Thinking.

THIAGARAJA

(1759 TO 1847)

With permission from Jaganmohan Palace, Mysore.

He inherited all the great virtues of his father such as, for instance, devotion * to God, steadfastness of purpose, and contentment. His benevolence of heart was of an active and real type as well as of non-impulsive and steady nature, quite unlike the passive and (I may say) false sympathy of Margaret who wept aloud on witnessing a murder-scene enacted at a Theatre and continued to sob even when, after the performance, she returned to her motor car; but who mercilessly kicked her chauffeur for his unreadiness to drive the car, even after her attention was drawn to the fact that the chauffeur's fever, suddenly caught at midnight, had pointed to 100 degrees.

Thiagaraja was, as we shall see, a little bit of occultist too. He loved, and even respected, his wife and paid a manly homage to her goodness and understanding as well as to her tenderness

* The Raja of Tanjore built 15 houses at Thiruvaiyar and offered them to 15 Vidwans of whom Rama Brahmam, Thiagaraja's father, was one. While the other 14 Vidwans gladly accepted their offers, Rama Brahmam alone declined his, with thanks. It is also said that he accepted his offer for the sake of courtesy but re-offered it to a really needy man. This shows Rama Brahmam's contentment which he transmitted to his son.

and beauty. He regarded his only daughter and, for that matter, his only child, Sitalakshmi by name, as the rarest treasure in the world. He had a grandson too, called by his own name but alas ! short-lived.

Good Homer, it is said, sometimes nods ; and the brightest sun and the whitest moon have each its own spot. So, from some one of his ancestors, our musician inherited impetuosity and irritability of temper, so much so, that, in spite of his being otherwise good. he was highly disagreeable to his disciples and would at times treat them with harshness. For instance, a certain boy was, according to the custom of the day, acting as a servant to Thiagaraja in return for the music he learnt. The guru used to scold him downright for delay in the services, such as getting things ready for pooja, as well as, in repeating the songs taught and would even belabour him soundly. One day the boy faced the guru and said to him point blank : " For my dullness in learning music, I may be cudgelled ; but for your quickness in losing temper, you certainly deserve thrashing." Straightaway he bolted.

Probably this was a typically bad boy. But under Thiagaraja there were some good boys too, who almost succeeded, not to irritate his sensitive nerves, but to please him in every way and who thus learnt all his songs and faithfully transmitted them down to our own day. Some of his more important disciples were :—

1. Ganesayya Garu,
2. Subbarama Bhagavathar,
3. Sojiri Sitharamiah,
4. Thiruvathiyur Kuppiah Garu,
5. Umayapuram Krishnier, } Brothers.
6. Umayapuram Sundrier, } Brothers.
7. Thillaisthanam Ramiengar,
8. Thiruvaiyar Aiyavier,
9. Nemam Subramaniah,
10. Nangavaram Nilakantiah,
11. Walajapet Venkataramana Bhagavathar,
12. Manambuchavadi VenkatasubbayyaGaru,
13. Kannayya Bhagavathar,
14. Amrithalingam Pillay.

Even these had some experience of harsh treatment at the hands of their guru. One evening a few of them intruded upon a marriage party in a village near Thiruvaiyar and eagerly listened to a dancing-girl's Javali, for which their guru had the greatest aversion. His pupils however liked it immensely and, on returning home, repeated it among themselves. Next morning, Thiagaraja came to know what had happened the previous day and vented his anger thus: "You Imps! To attend a marriage uninvited and without my permission is itself a fault; to see there a dancing-girl is an offence; to hear her sing a lascivious Javali is a sin; but to make bold to repeat it inside my roof and to my hearing........what shall I say?" Forthwith the *imps* were driven out and had to forego their morning meal. Probably they would have been starved the whole day, had not the saintly wife of the guru had the kindness and courage to intercede on their behalf.

"Is not tenderness a requisite quality in a guru?" asked the wife.

"Is not true tenderness a well-timed correction?" replied the guru.

"Should correction be attended with loss of temper?" asked, again, the wife.

"Does not the thorn grow along with the rose?" retorted the guru.

"But do not the people pluck the rose and chuck the thorn away?" was the crushing reply of the wife.

"Ah! my dear wife!", confessed the guru "you have indeed corrected me. True it is that he only may chastise who loves. One may have controlled one's senses; become an expert in Vedanta, been blessed with wife, wealth, and children; have acquired the merit of japathapa; performed many a Yaga ; attained reputation as an excellent reader of other men's thoughts ; and gained popularity as a Bhagavathar; but if that one has not learnt to preserve tranquility of mind, happiness is ever denied to that short-tempered one. Hence, no peace, no joy."

This happy idea inculcated in his Sama Krithi —*Shanthamuleka*—may be regarded as a turning-point in his life, as having enabled him to finally triumph over his weakness of irascibility. Even if it did not, his sensitive nature need not blur our vision. For, did not Rousseau, while he succeeded to educate the whole world through his *Emile*, miserably failed to educate his own children, on account of his irascibility? Why, was not Beethoven characterised as an "ill-natured churlish being?" When, in one of his performances, a noble and a lady conversed somewhat audibly; did he not lose his temper, stop suddenly and shout: "To such pigs I play no more"? When, again, his own brother boastfully called himself in a private letter—a Land-owner; did he not angrily retort that he was a Brain-owner? Yet, the whole of Europe has long regarded both Rousseau and Beethoven as two great luminaries of European 'education' and 'music' respectively. Prudence and greatness run in opposite directions; and irascibility has nothing to do with greatness any more than a flowing beard or twirled moustache. Would you throw away a ripe pine apple, on account of the roughness of its coat? Do you not enjoy the beauty of the moon, despite its dark spot? Indeed man is a bundle of contradictory qualities, on account of the tug-of-war between the natural and moral forces that are in him; and a consistency, even in appearance, could not be attained but by long habits of philosophical discipline, which our musician got only in the latter part of his life.

As regards Thiagaraja's method of teaching, there is no doubt that he adopted the ancient Lip-Ear Method. He divided his disciples into several groups and taught each group a different set of his krithis. For, he found it not only impossible but also undesirable to teach all his pupils all his krithis. It is said that most of his disciples did not attain Swara-gnanam; nor did the guru wish them to attain it, lest they should, with their supposed originality, tamper with *his* way of singing. Further, like a true teacher that he was, he had the genius to discover the ancient advice, viz. "Given a stupid boy, make him an efficient worker" contained the whole secret of education; that the clever must be dismissed from the teacher's calculations and the main, if not the sole, figure in the field of education must be the stupid boy; that any fool with a knowledge bottled in him could pour it to a clever boy but it needed the skilled workman to be able to *teach* a dull boy; and that, just as the man who could not find his way in lanes and by-paths was no guide, the man who could not teach the stupid boy was no teacher at all. With a set purpose, therefore, he chose for his pupils ordinary boys and used all his skill and cleverness to make the best of them and convert them from dull drones into efficient workers and propagators of his krithis. Well did he choose so; for, the world wants, for its daily routine business, jutka horses and not circus horses.

CHAPTER IX

PERIODS OF HIS CAREER

(a) *First Period.*

THIAGARAJA'S career, as musical composer, falls into four periods, viz, those of bigotry, tolerance, philosophy and altruism. We need not be surprised at his early period of bigotry which, it is said, cites conscience and the name of God as the basis of its acts. The bigoted Protestants persecuted the Catholics only in God's name; while in the same God's name, the bigoted Catholics perpetrated all the atrocities of the Spanish Inquisition. Again, the bigoted Tippu carried a sword in one hand and the Koran in the other, only to please his God; while, to please their own Gods, the Crusaders and the Turks cut each other's throats. When, therefore, Thiagaraja selected Rama in preference to all other gods and sang;—

1. Ela Dayaradu,
2. Oorage Kalkuna,
3. Rama Kothandarama,
4. Ramam Bhajeham,

and a host of other songs exclusively in praise of Rama; he was, if not dogmatically, yet devotionally bigoted. He did not wilfully prevent any further light from entering his mind; but no light happened to enter there for a time. "Just as the *kar* paddy is inferior to the *samba* paddy; a lamp light to a torch light; a canal to the Cauvery; a lotus to the full moon; a man, however charming, to Manmatha; a lake to an ocean; so, all the Gods in this world are, O! Rama! inferior to you,"—thus he cried in his, *Koruvelpulu* song. He was superstitious to the core and performed rituals and ceremonial worship with an almost petrifying accuracy, as appears in his *Koluvamregada.* The idol-worship, especially the worship of his own golden idol, was to him the only means of attaining salvation. He would rise early every morning, bathe in the ever-running water of the Cauvery, cause his pet idol to be bathed in rose water, give it milk to drink and sing devotional songs to the accompaniment of a *thambura.* If need be, he would then go round the town on oonchvritti business. Otherwise he would employ the time in teaching his disciples new songs. At about 12 Noon, he would bathe again, entertain Rama with an excellent dinner of six savours, give him betel with scented nut, repeat the same process in the night, burn camphor before him, charm him by singing beautiful and sublime ragas and lull him thereby to sleep on soft bed of sweet flowers. He composed distinct songs for each of the above-mentioned functions, as for instance, *Aragimpave* for the offering of milk and food and *Vidamusayave* for the offering of betel. The whole night, except a few hours of inevitable sleep, he would spend in bhajana, singing old, or improvising new, songs.

Such was the intensity of his bigotry that when one day the goddess of Thiruvaiyar, Dharmasamvardhani, was taken in procession round the town, he ran quickly into his house and stood, like a child, before his Rama, that he might avoid seeing the Saivite Goddess who, in his opinion, failed criminally—as the presiding deity of the town—to check the growing wickedness of the people and contrasted her with his own household god, Rama, of whose wholesome influence upon himself he was deeply conscious. In his krithi, *Lavanyarama*, he characterised the Saivite Goddess as belonging to the school of Ignorance: "O! Charming Rama! let me see thee to the delectation of my eyes. O! Moon to the Kumuda of Lakshmi's mind! O! Thou who art a hundred Manmathas rolled into one! Thy mind, thy joy and thy ways do differ from those of the Deity of the School of Ignorance[1]. What, then, is that deity for?"

Within two decades of his stay at Thiruvaiyar, Thiagaraja felt mighty change had been taking place in the condition of the town and its surroundings. The people were rudely disturbed by the political convulsions wherewith the East India Company was shaking the country. Their intense faith in God and their noble spirit of sacrifice were slowly giving way to gross materialism and worship of Mammon. Their brows that used to look up to heaven began to kiss the ground. The unfeeling train of trade usurped the land and dispossessed the swain. Hence Thiagaraja exclaimed in his Denuka song ; *Thelialeru Rama* : O ! Rama ! the people do not know the right path to faith, but would rather go about the earth and create confusion. Though again they get up in the morning, bathe in water, besmear their bodies with sacred ashes and pose as praiseworthy men; they manifest an inordinate lust for money rather than, O ! Rama !, desire for your grace." Later on, he even felt sad that he lived at Thiruvaiyar,

1. Thamasamatha Deiva.

where wealth accumulated and men decayed and, in despair, sang: *Tholinejesina*—"O ! my God ! I now understand the fruits of my karma; for, despite my repeated worship, you continue to be what you were, leaving me severely alone. Again, you have—perhaps to lower me in the estimation of my contemporaries --dropped me into a town bereft of Haridasas but full of Epicureans."

Soon after, as chance would have it, Thiagaraja fell ill and failed to see, as was his wont, Rama in his nocturnal dreams. This calamity, as he called it, he forthwith attributed to the wrath of Dharmasamvardhani, lamented his abuse of her and advised himself much in the strain of Parnell :—

"Where you can't unriddle, learn to trust".

Thus changed in spirit, he, for the first time, burst into a Saivite song—*Karunajoodavamma*: "O! Queen to Chandrakaladhara! Peerless Mistress of the town of Panchanada! Dharmasamvardhani! Pray, look at me with a merciful eye. I now believe that you alone can save man from the consequences of his evil deeds, done in ignorant pride. I now perceive no difference between Rama, Siva and Yourself. O! Queen!

abandon me not." To further please the Goddess, he had to sing of her Lord too. The ice was thus broken; and the first period of bigotry gave way to the second period of tolerance, to which he was drawn by yet another force, viz, his venerable wife's unaccountable predilection for Parashakthi.

(b) *Second Period.*

In the second period, he sang of all deities and made absolutely no difference between god and god. For example, *Girirajasutha* related to Ganesa; *Neevanti Deivamu* to Subramanya; *Sambo Mahadeva* to Siva; *Prananathabirana* to Krishna; *Pahiramadootha* to Hanuman; and *Thulasi jagajjanani* to the thulasi plant. The last song was a translation, in terms of Thiagaraja's own Krithi, of a well-known Sanskrit verse [1]:—

यन्मूलेसर्वतीर्थानि यन्मध्ये सर्वदेवताः ।
यदग्रे सर्ववेदाश्च तुलसींत्वां नमाम्यहम् ॥

Thiagaraja, be it noted, had a genius, which he often utilised, for quickly translating any verse in terms of his own krithi. While he was thus pouring his improvised songs in praise of whatsoever gods he chanced upon, his shrewd disciples assi-

1 "I bow to you, Thulasi, in whose root remain all the sacred waters, in whose centre all the Devas, and in whose head all the Vedas."

duously drank the nectar of music, conveyed by them, without ever questioning the form of their guru's worship; for, such enquiry would, as they full well knew, be like "questioning the paper upon which a king's message was written.'

About this time, there occurred four incidents in seriatim, which effected a perceptible change in Thiagaraja's angle of vision and sent him on to the third period of his career.

At last, free himself from his confinement in his native place he did and set out on a travel to some of the more important religious centres of South India. At the special request of his Walajapet disciple, Venkatramana Bhagavathar, he first went to Thirupathi via Walajapet. There he found a screen intervening between him and the God Venkateswara, just as, in times of yore, Nanda found a bull intervening between him and Thiruppangur Siva. He feelingly sang, *Therathiyogarada:* "O! Venkataramana of Thirupathi! Will you no cause the screen of jealousy that obstructs from within, to move aside? I now feel as much miserable as one whose food, at the time of taking it, has been spoiled by dirty flies; *or* as one whose mind, at the time of contemplating Hari, wanders along a Pariah lane." Forthwith the screen, as did the bull, moved aside ; and the God presented Himself in all His radiant glory to the sincere Bhaktha.

First Incident.

Kovoor, near Poonamalle, was the next place to which he repaired, where he dedicated his extempore songs—

(1). *Nammivachina*
(2). *Korisevimpare*
(3). *Ye Vasudanivanti*

to the Siva God. There he met one Sundaresa Mudaliar, a Tamil Scholar and Patron of Music, who received our musician with all respect, form, and formality. But Thiagaraja at once diagnosed that there was something afflicting Mudaliar's mind.

"What afflicts you?" asked Thiagaraja. "This is not the original place intended for your reception," confessed Sundaresa Mudaliar, "and the present arrangements are but a make-shift. I had made grand preparations to accord you a fitting reception and thus to tread in the footsteps of my ancestors."

"But, " interrupted Thiagaraja, "I am not a King, nor any one of King's men, for you to think of giving me a fitting reception. I am but an ordinary mortal, a foot pilgrim, a beggar too unskilful to fawn or flatter for wealth here, but mad to ask of Heaven what the generality of the people have recently learnt not to prize, viz, truth, wisdom, grace and peace."

"I am one of those," continued Mudaliar, "who are firmly convinced that every member of our society should be honored in proportion as he is necessary; and I am bold enough to say that Bhagavathars, like you, are more necessary for a State than even a King. If a country is fortunate enough to have able and willing preachers like you, O! the routine business of the Government can be carried on even by puppets. A breath can make or unmake a king; but a bold preacher or a sweet singer cannot be made, or supplied, to order. We have heard of "King-Makers"; but have there ever been Bhagavathar-Makers or Musician-Makers? Further, in the upheaval of the present state of society, caused by the aggressive policy of foreigners, I fear the most important emotional side of education will be neglected and the overbearing intellectual side brought to the forefront. Your krithis, I feel in my heart of hearts, are ordained by God to set. both the sides of education in equilibrium at last. My ancestors have taught me, both by precept and example, that preachers and musicians, like you, are more important than even kings. Hence my anxiety to accord you a fitting reception. But God altered what I had proposed. Look yonder, please, at the fire which has consumed all the materials I had gathered." So saying, he burst into a Tamil verse—

> பாரோர் பலரைச் சபை கூட்டி நாளும் பஜனை செய்தும்
> பேராகிய பிள்ளையார் பிடிக்கக் குரங்கானது போல்
> சீராரிராம! செயல் வேறுபட்ட இத்தீங்கினை யான்
> ஆரோடு சொல்லுவன் ! கோபால! நீயருள்வாய்சிறிதே.[1]

Thiagaraja's sympathy followed Mudaliar's emotion ; and when requested to sing, the guest quickly translated the Tamil verse in terms of his own krithi ; *Evarithonedelpudu* and sang it: "To whom shall I, O ! Rama ! represent my difficulty ? My bhajana has produced an opposite effect, as per the proverb '*I wanted to produce a Genesa but a monkey came forth.*' O ! Gopala ! to whom shall I represent my difficulty ?" This Manavathi song astounded Mudaliar to such a degree that he at once ordered his servants to bring a palanquin and placed in a corner thereof a purse of Rs. 1,000.

---

[1] For the translation of this Tamil verse, see lines 4 to 9 in the same page from the bottom :—"To whom, etc., difficulty ?"

Second Incident.

It was 5 o'clock in the morning when Thiagaraja resumed his journey. Four bearers, two on either side, carried the palanquin which contained our musician, quite unaware of the purse placed therein. All on a sudden, within an hour's journey, fell upon the palanquin—not the expected rays of the Sun—but an unexpected shower of stones. Thiagaraja's disciples saw at a distance a crowd of armed men approaching and cried 'Thieves !' Startled by the outcry, the guru got down and said: "I have not a single pie with me: you had better take this palanquin, if you please." The disciples interrupted ; "Master ! Sundaresa Mudaliar placed a purse of Rs. 1,000 on the palanquin and bade us keep silence." At once Thiagaraja took and flang the purse in the direction of the thieves saying: "Here is your money ; take it." The Chief of the thieves fell at the musician's feet and replied "No, Sir, it is yours ; and ourselves are from this moment yours."

"But why did you hurl stones at us ?," asked Thiagaraja.

Of course, to get at the purse," replied the Chief, " but I confess we have been taught by necessity to thieve. Even during my father's time, I noted that health and plenty cheered the labouring swain. But O! what a mighty revolution in these few years! I feel, all around, the grip of a tyrant's hand; and a tyrant within a tyrant is all the art I learnt in my life. O! the perverseness of human nature which condemns in public what it encourages in secret!"

"Now you speak words of wisdom," interrupted Thiagaraja.

"There's reason for that;" continued the Chief, "as my comrades threw stones at the palanquin, I slang a big stone aimed straight at you. But lo! it returned upon myself and caused a big wound on my forehead. I tried to find out the cause, when two young, strong, and fair warriors dazzled my eyes with the effulgent beauty of their handsome youth and dumbfounded me by the skilful use of their bows. "Who are you both?," I asked. They whispered to me "We are insignificant pupils of this great guru," pointing to you. I was going to ask for their names and put them other questions. But suddenly they were lost to my sight. If you are the *great guru* of these two angels, all of us shall cease thieving hereafter and become your ever obedient pupils. Pray, Sir, tell me who those angels are."

Thiagaraja's mind became upset; and he felt keenly pained to think that the two angels —possibly Rama and Lakshmana—who had condescended to show themselves to a thief, were not kind enough to do *him* the same favour. He at once sang *Mundutenuka* in Durbar: "O! the Destroyer of Mura and Khara! Come, come on either side of me, in front and behind me. Raghunandana! Where am I going to witness a beauty like yours? O! Moon that rose out of the ocean of Ravikula! Come soon with your Kothanda, along with Lakshmana."

The Chief learnt the angels to be Rama and Lakshmana. The thousand rupees were presented to the new converts; and they offered to carry the palanquin. Thiagaraja accepted their service and resumed his journey. While the whilom thieves, as they carried, sang the palanquin song; the musician inside improvised *Ramabana* and *Evarichirira*, in praise of the great bow, wherewith Rama astounded the Chief of the thieves.

Conjeevarem was the next place of visit; and a Madhyamavati song, *Vinayakunivalenu*, was dedicated to the goddess Kamatchi there. From Conjeevarem to Madhyarjunam was a pretty long journey of about 200 miles. From one of the many villages through which the palanquin-bearers had to pass, a loud cry issued. It was then 6 A. M.

"Halt!" ordered Thiagaraja, "we shall stay here for the day. But what is that cry about? You Chief! run and bring me news of it."

Third Incident.

The Chief at once mixed himself with the crowd in front of a temple there; got all the necessary information and related it thus to his new guru:—"A certain pilgrim to Thirupathi, who was accompanied by his wife and child, missed his way and, by chance, reached this village last night between 9 and 10. He found all the doors bolted, as usual, at that hour, since otherwise tigers and other wild animals from the neighbouring jungles would attack the inmates thereof. The pilgrim seems to have knocked all the doors; but none of them opened. He then knocked the temple door; but again no response came. To save his innocent wife and the devine-looking baby from the jaws of man-eaters, he climbed up the temple-wall in order to reach the door and open it from inside, but lo! when he dropped, from the wall, inside the temple, he fell into a deep well and was killed.

"Peace! Peace! Peace!" ejaculated Thiagaraja. "The wife," continued the Chief, "not knowing what had happened inside, kept calling to her husband the whole night; and perhaps her calling kept the night-prowlers at bay. The day dawned and the temple door was opened. In ran the eager wife only to find her husband floating on the water. Soon the body was brought out of the temple and placed there where you now see the crowd. The cry is the wife's wail."

Thiagaraja ran to the spot, passed his right hand along the whole body of the pilgrim, kneeled down, prayed fervently for his revival and sang—not *Najivadhara* in Bilahari as is traditionally handed down—but *Sri Rama Padama* in Amrithavahini. For, as Mr. L. Muthiah Bhagavathar of Harikesanellore rightly observed, the Bilahari krithi could not be the song for the occasion, beause the Bilahari Raga has never been reputed to have the power of reviving the dead body and also because there is nothing in the song alluding even indirectly to the incident described. On the other hand, Amirithavahini has ever been, as the name itself indicates, just the Raga to revive the dead body; and the meaning of the song directly relates to the incident referred to—"O; valiant Hero? You saw on the way Ahalya unable to bear her stony form and ever shedding tears; and you protected her by restoring her to her original form. Help (this man) in the same way (by restoring him to life)."

The pilgrim got up as if from sleep and resumed his journey to Thirupathi, along with his wife and child, after partaking the refreshments served by the people of the village. We are here reminded of a puranic story in which Abboothi's son was revived by the fervent prayer of Thirunavukkarasu, as well as of a historical fact that Humayun recovered from his illness by the genuine wish of his father, Babar.

Before those who may seriously object to these miracles being recorded here, we place what a great writer of the present century thought it worth his while to state in his book: "Miracles are but productions of physical phenomena by occult means. What was a miracle at one period of history becomes a common occurrence at a later time. The occult sciences of mediaeval days are the mothers of modern sciences. When Jesus and his disciples performed wonderful cures, the people thought they were great teachers, because they used unknown forces. The same miracles are performed to-day by sciences; and they excite no wonder now. When, again, King Edward VII, then Prince of Wales, visited India; a wonder-worker performed the well-known basket-trick, which we witness even now oft and on. An expert mind can so dwell upon an image as to cause, within its own photosphere, that image to appear; and it can be so intesified that everyone looking upon the person producing the picture, can see nothing but that picture. The mental image is impressed upon the minds of the spectators with such intensity that it cannot be distinguished from the reality. This miracle is caused by the force of the expert mind. Again, within a short time after death, life may be restored by any one who understands the process of restoration. The Electrotherapist has, on rare occasions, resurrected the lifeless body by the use of electricity. The difference between the Occutlists' method and the Electrotherapists' method is, the former does the work through mental process, while the latter by the aid of an electric battery. In the course of the evolution of the human race, to triumph over premature death will cease to be a miracle. But from time immemmorial, there have been rare occultists whose touch, coupled with their trained will-power, has resurrected many a dead body."

If true, Thiagaraja might have been one of them.

In gratitude, our musician sang the Bilahari song too; stayed in the village till afternoon; and then left it for Madhyarjunam, where he worshipped Mahalingaswami. He then moved to a neighbouring village, Govindapuram, and paid a visit to the Mutt of Bohendraswami *alias* Sadguruswami of Namasiddhanta fame. To another neighbouring village, Thiruvisinellore, he hied and paid his respects to the name of Sridhara Venkatacharyar *alias* Aiyaval, who was reputed to have brought the Ganjes to his village. From Thiruvisinellore he turned eastward and reached Nagpur, the modern Negapatam, presided over by Nilayadakshi, wife of Kayarohana. There, to his utter disappointment, he found what Oliver Goldsmith had done in Italy—

> " Contrasted faults through all men's manners reign,
> Though poor, luxurious; though submissive, vain;
> Though grave yet trifling; zealous yet untrue;
> And even in penance, planning sins anew."

And the music prevailing at Nagpur during the time of his visit was in the same freezing point as it had been delineated by Kalamegha

"வாழ்த்து திருநாகை வாகான தேவடியாள்
பாழ்த்த குரலெடுத்துப் பாடினாள்—நேற்றுக்
கழுதை கெட்டவண்ணான் கண்டேன் கண்டேனென்றுப்
பழுதை யெடுத்தோடி வந்தான் பார்."[1]

He felt sorry he had visited Nagpur and attributed his disappointment to his past Karma in a Saveri song, *Karmame Balavanthamaye*: "After all (my) Karma has won the day.[2] O! Wife to Kayarohana! Nilayadakshi of Nagpur! I got out to travel and appeared before your holy presence, only to find out remedies wherewith to cure the wealthy of their vanities and other ills. But (inasmuch as disappointment was my reward) Karma has had its day." Upon Nagpur he turned his back and left it for Rameswaram and Dhanushkoti, in the latter of which he sang *Kotinadulu*. From hence he went westward to Madura, where he sang *Manasunilpa* in Abogi and then moved north-

---

1. The dancing-girl of the prosperous city of Negapatam was beautiful to look at but very ugly in singing—so ugly that the washerman of the place mistook her music for the braying of the ass, he had missed the day before, and came running with a long stick.

2. Literally—"become strong."

ward to Srirangam, where he sang O! *Rngasayi*; *Karunajoodavayya*; and *Rajuvedalu*. After a pretty long stay, he left Srirangam for Thiruvaiyar and thus finished his not-uneventful pilgrimage.

Now that his journey came to an end, Thiagaraja had time to ruminate over its various incidents that crowded into his mind, especially, those of Sundaresa Mudaliar's verse, the stone shower and the temple-calamity. He first cogitated the new idea supplied by Mudaliar and felt that he was hitherto familiar only with such verses and songs as had addressed themselves to one God at a time and that the idea of addressing a plurality of Gods simultaneously in one and the same verse or song was to him a novel one. He therefore dicussed with himself his krithi, *Evarithoneaelpudu*, wherein two gods, Rama and Gopala, had been addressed. Doubts arose in his mind as to which of these two gods, or even which others, should, intelligently and by a process of ratiocination, be chosen. He went on philosophising and imperceptibly glided into the third period of his career. The stone-shower incident rivetted his attention upon Rama, but for whose timely help he would have been mortally wounded. And the temple-calamity further encouraged him to lean on Rama, as it was that deity, as the presiding God of the village, who responded to his Amrithavahini song.

Fourth Incident.

Meanwhile, a fourth incident came to pass, which set at rest the wavering mind of Thiagaraja and confirmed him finally in the new position he had taken. A learned Brahmin of Benares who, on his way to Rameswaram, halted at Thiruvaiyar, happened to deliver, on the solicitations of the people, a short discourse on "Avathars," in connection with which he reviewed the opening passage of the fourth Chapter of Bhagavad Gita. Thiagaraja was present. The learned Brahmin spoke to his eager audience about five points, namely :—

(1) Whether the Avathars are of free-choice or Karma-determined.

(2) Whether they are real or illusory,

(3) What is the proper time for them ?

(4) What is their purpose ?

(5) What is the nature of the body assumed by them ?

After a rapid sketch of the first four points, the learned lecturer waxed more eloquent when he approached the fifth. Indeed, in his fervid enthusiasm, he forgot himself and, identifying himself with the subject, addressed the hearers thus :

"Regarding the nature of the Body assumed by avathars, our Lord said: 'In the way the creatures of the world resort to me, in that way do I serve them.' Scientists agree to state that the world began with the watery age. Valmiki only confirmed the statement when he observed: सर्वंसालिलमेवासीत् 'Everything was exclusively water.' While thus the whole *prapancha* was full, and indeed made up, of water, what sort of animals could possibly live therein other than water-animals? Hence our Lord assumed the form of *Mathsya* (Fish) in order to serve those water-animals in the way in which they resorted to Him. Later on, the water dried up and the land appeared. Forth came a new set of animals which lived both on land and in water such as the tortoise. Hence the Lord became a *Koorma* (Tortoise) and thereby served the water-land-animals, in the way in which they resorted to Him. The third species of animals, it is said, was the Mammalian group, such as boar and elephant. Hence the avathar *Varaha* (Boar)

Then, man evolved himself out of beasts but yet retained many of the beastly qualities, quite justifying Bharthrihari's dictum :

मनुष्यरूपेणमृगाश्चरन्ति ।

'Beasts roam in the form of men ?' Hence the avathar *Narasimma* (Man-Lion). Later on, the beast in man shed itself, till at last he learnt to crush all the beastly qualities with his feet. Hence the avathar *Vamana* (Symbol of man) crushed down Bali (symbol of beast) with his feet. Now, man shone for a time as the noblest creation of God. Reaction then set in. The beastly qualities once again got the upper hand; and the Kshatriyas, especially, began to be a menace to society. Hence *Parasurama* came and tried to teach them, by fear, a lesson as to how they should conduct themselves in the world. But the experiment failed. Hence *Sri Rama* appeared and taught them the same lesson, not by fear, but by love and example. All that *Sri Krishna* did was to give Arjuna a code of precepts of which his previous avathar was a personal example. Since example is better than precept, Sri Rama is a safer guide than Sri Krishna. Further, of all the multifarious gods of India, Siva and Vishnu are, by common consent, the chosen ones. Rama represents both Siva and Vishnu, inasmuch as his very name consists of the Jiva (life-giving) letters of Vishnu and Siva manthras, viz., "Ra" and "Ma." Hence all the Gods are focussed in Rama. Just as all the waters that fall from heaven reach, though through different rivers, the same ocean; so all the prayers that fall from the lips of man reach, though through different gods, the same Rama.'.

(c) Third Period.

Thiagaraja, who was all attention to the lecture, could not contain himself but burst into an epoch-making song *Evarani Nirnayinchirira*; "O! God! How do the wise men determine as to who thou art and how do they worship Thee? (Do they worship thee) as Siva, Vishnu, Brahma or Parabrahma? 'Ma' is the Jiva of Sivamanthra and 'Ra' of Vishnumanthra. To the noble person that knew this secret (and ably taught it to me) I humbly bow."

This 'epoch-making' song, besides being an adequate expression of Thiagaraja's gratitude to the preacher, inaugurates his third period of philosophy. Whereas, in the first period, he thought of Rama but ignored all other gods; whereas, in the second period, he thought alike of all the gods; now in the third period, he learnt to concentrate and focus all the gods in Rama. *Dwaitamusukhama* and *Ethavunna*, for instance, belong to this period.

(d) Fourth Period.

It was at the very end of his life that Thiagaraja approached the fourth period of his career, to which we shall refer later on.

CHAPTER X

HIS VIEWS OF MUSIC.

THIAGARAJA'S views of Music stand reflected in many of his krithis, such as, for instance,

(1) *Mokshmugalada*,
(2) *Sangithasasthragnanamu*,
(3) *Ragasusdharasa*,
(4) *Anandasagaramu*,
and (5) *Endukupeddala*,

In the first, he raised a weighty question—"Can there be *Moksha* or salvation for an unmusical being?" Here no less a personage than Yagnavalkya backed up Thiagaraja by ruling in his Smrithi "whoever knows the secrets of Vina-play; whoever is an adept in the matter of Sruthi; whoever is well-versed in Thala; he does easily get into the way of *Moksha*."[1] In the second, our musician gave us a rationale for his query, viz, "the knowledge of the science of music yields the joy of Sarupya."

---

1. वीणावादनतत्वज्ञः श्रुतिजातिविशारदः ।
तालज्ञंश्चाप्रयासेनमोक्षमार्गंगच्छति ॥

But what is Sarupya? As four important milestones of salvation, our sacred works have marked Salokya, Samipya, Sarupya; and Sayujya. The smaller souls, Jivatmas, after a very long and even tire- some course of slow evolution, acquire ability to have a happy glimpse of theGreat Soul, Paramatma, though from at a distance. This is the first stage, called Salokya. By a further process of evolution, they are able to approach nearer and nearer the Great soul, till at last they find themselves side by side with Him. This is the second stage, called Samipya. By a still further process of evolution, they learn to shed their peculiar shapes and angularities and assume the same *rupa* or form as that of the Great soul. This is the third stage, called Sarupya. Because of the sameness of rupa, now reached, the Jivatmas and the Paramatma find it very easy to merge in, or unite with, each other, as fire with fire or air with air. When they thus do effect the union, the Jivatmas are deemed to have attained the fourth and last stage, called Sayujya [1]

1. The reader will note that the *Kalpura-Diparadhana* or Camphor Burning before God is intended to illustrate, and daily bring home to the mind of the masses, the vital truth of this ancient theory. The camphor is the Jivatma and the agni is Paramatma. When both meet, the camphor sheds its own form and becomes one with agni; and then both disappear.

Now a question arises as to what is the *rupa* or form of the Great Soul which the smaller souls must assume before merging in it. Our philosophy begins with a premise that God is Sound and He is *Nada*.

Compare—

(1) The Vedic authority—"Sabda Nishtam Jagad."

(2) The Biblical authority—"In the beginning was the word; and the word was with God; and the word was God."

(3) Thiagaraja's Chitharanjani song—"Nadathanumanisam."

(4) Tagore's *Gitanjali*—"O! God! I know that only as a singer I come before thy presence".

(5) Sri Sankaracharyar's *Sivanandalahari*—"Sarupyam Thava poojane Sivamahadevethi Sankirthane".

(6) Sarangadev's *Sangitharatnakara*—"Vande Nadathanum".

Hence the smaller souls which are to mix themselves with the great soul to attain salvation must, as a condition-precedent, assume the same form of sound as that of the Great Soul. In other words, music is a necessary and indispensable *sine qua non* to every blessed individual smaller soul which must therefore possess or acquire a reasonable degree of susceptibility thereto. All need not sing but shall hear singing. Otherwise there is no salvation. Hence it was that Thiagaraja instinctively sang *Mokshamugalada.* 'Ragasudharasa' speaks of music as capable of giving its votary all the fruits of Yaga, Yoga, Thiaga and Bhoga. 'Anandasagaramu' blackmarks all unmusical beings as so many burdens to the earth. And 'Endukupeddala' lays down a curriculm of studies and includes music therein.

CHAPTER XI

HIS WORKS ON MUSIC.

BESIDES Krithis, which alone were sufficient to immortalise his name, our musician composed Kirthanas as well. He was, again, responsible for five more works, viz., Divyanamavali, Ragarathnamalika, Bhakthavijayam, Nowkacharithram and Pancharatna.

The first forms a body of very simple songs intended to help the veriest tyro to worship God with sweet voice which He likes. The second consists of one hundred kirthanas in one hundred ragas, beginning with *Ragarathnamalikache* in Ritigowla. Both these works have been rightly merged in the main work of Thiagaraja.

The third, viz. Bhakthavijayam, forms a body of devotional kirthanas composed for the purpose of deep contemplation and worship. The full name of the work is "Prahlada Bhakthavijayam." If the songs found therein were dedicated to Prahlada, we should have no remark to make. But if they purported to have been sung by Prahlada, or in other words, if Thiagaraja ever meant to put the forty-five songs of Bhakthavijayam into the mouth of Prahlada; then, our musician must be deemed to have commited the mistake of anachronism, even from the Puranic point of view. The reader will note that almost all the songs of Bhakthavijayam address themselves invariably to Rama as for instance—

(1) *Rama, Abhirama,*

and (2) *Thamasmela Sitamanoramana.*

Prahlada knew only the first four avathars and could not therefore even dream of the future Rama. Again, we see no reason why these two score and five songs should still remain under a separate category and why they should not be merged in our musician's main work, as has been the case with his Divyanamavali and Ragarathnamalika.

But 'Nowkacharithram' has its own tale to tell and deserves an independent classification. It narrates the story of an excursion, in a pleasure-boat on the Jumna, of the Gopis of Brindavan in company with Lord Krishna. A terrible storm tossed the boat furiously and threatened to drown it. The Gopis prayed to Krishna for help but in vain; for, the waters were rising and making their way into the boat. They came through some new cracks that opened at the bottom. The Gopis screamed: *Allakallolamaye*. With a stern voice, however, did Sri Krishna order: "Fill the cracks with your garments." The helpless women resigned themselves to the will of the Lord. Suddenly the whole scene changed; and the Gopis found themselves safe on the banks of the Jumna with their garments. Their joy knew no bounds. The songs of Nowkacharithram are of a simple type of melody; and Mr. Thirumalayya Naidu compares them to Handel's *Water-Music*, which was performed by a party of musicians in a boat which followed King George I in his barge down the Thames, the object being to appease the royal hearer's wrath.

With regard to the origin of *Pancharatna*, Govinda Marar's* memorable meeting with Thiagaraja has to be related. In the early part of the 19th century, there lived in Travancore—Ramamangalam of Moovattupuai Taluq— a famous musician, called Govinda Marar, whose date has been found to be approximately 1798 to 1843. He was small in stature but big in fame and afflicted with rheumatism which made him a cripple for

* Since M . Lakshmana Pillay and I have each independently got from the same Vedadrisadasa Mudaliar the information of Govinda Marars meeting with Thiagaraja who had got it from his own uncle that was bodily present at that meeting, any tradition to the contrary or giving any other name, such as Kesaviah, must be brushed aside.

life, but endowed with extraordinary powers which made him a celebrity for life and even after. He used to sing with a thambura in one hand and a kanjira in the other; so self-contained a musician was he. His thambura had seven strings, unlike the four-stringed thambura of to-day, consisting of 3 saranis, 3 panchamas and 1 mandra. His unique thambura had a flag of challenge attached to it. We hear of a similar instrument having been used by Peria Vythi who, in his best days, travelled in a palanquin and

> "High placed in hall, a welcome guest,
> He pour'd to lord and lady gay
> The unpremeditated lay,"

But the voice of even the Sivaganga musician could not reach the high pitch of the Travancorean's special instrument. Govinda Marar's *forte* was pallavi-singing in *shadkala* or six degrees of time; and he was therefore called "Shadkala Govindan."

The Shadkala system of singing pallavi may be described thus : A man who sings on the second degree, comprises the pallavi into half the space of time which he took to sing it on the first degree. To sing it again on the third degree, he would have to compress it into one-fourth of the same time; and so on up to the sixth degree. But the ordinary powers of the human voice are such as cannot permit any musician to sing a pallavi on the sixth degree, unless the first degree of time is extraordinarily slow. Again, the powers of measuring and regulating the first slow degree of time by a mere mental estimate will be heavily taxed and tested to the utmost limit. So volatile, unsubstantial and evanescent is time that, unless a reasonably short interval is allowed between two beatings its measurement is likely to elude the grasp of even the subtlest intellect. To be a successful Shadkala-singer of pallavi, one must be able to sing it either at an electric speed or at an extraordinarily slow speed. Govinda Marar adopted the second method; and there he was terrible to his rivals.

This celebrated Govinda Marar heard of the more celebrated Thiagaraja and wanted to meet him Nalla Thambi Mudaliar, keeper of the Royal Stables of Trivandrum, took him all the way to Thiruvaiyar, where the historic meeting of the two great men took place in 1838. What a glorious sight must that meeting have been! It was as if Shakespeare and Milton *or* Tasso and

Dante *or* Kalidasa and Kamban met together. The famous "squint-eyed" Vadivelu was also present there. Thiagaraja's private friend, Annachi Rayar, lodged them in a convenient building and attended to their other comforts. The same night at 8 o'clock, Thiagaraja and his disciples sat together on the small pial of his humble cottage with a castor-oil lamp acting as a representative of the departed sun. The people of Thiruvaiyar and the surrounding parts had already assembled in large numbers in front of the musician's house. The disciples began to sing. Meanwhile Govinda Marar, Nalla Thambi Mudaliar and Vadivelu went there, paid their namaskaras, and squatted. A grim silence followed the disciples' music; and none dared to break it.

Thiagaraja, like Haridas Swami of Brindavan, used to sing only when his inner Voice commanded ; and none of his disciples, therefore, would dare to ask him to sing. When, however Govinda Marar boldly requested Thiagaraja to sing, a sensation of surprise ran throughout the audience. Thiagaraja himself was taken aback and ejaculated: "Who is this person that can ask me to sing? Further, how can he expect an old man of 79 to sing to order?"

"If you are not disposed," replied Vadivelu "I shall ask Marar to sing,"

"What is a rheumatic patient, that he seems to be, going to sing?" asked Thiagaraja.

"A little," was Vadivelu's reply.

Thiagaraja nodded his head as if he wanted to hear that *little*.

Quite unaffected by whatever had transpired in his very presence, the "short-fingered" Govinda Marar readily took his thambura, which itself attracted enough notice, and began his ragamalika —alapana. *Thodi* was the first raga he elaborated. At once a great king, decked in all his regal glory and parading the pomp and circumstance of his lofty position, appeared to stalk before the audience. The singer changed the raga to *Asaveri*. Lo! that king was deposed from his throne of power and immersed in a sea of grief. *Kirvani* was sung next. A sage it was that, with a serene mind, sat in a lonely forest and calmly contemplated the beauty of nature. Thus did Govinda Marar play on the emotions of his hearers. He knew what phase, temper, circumstance or condition of life, high or low, serious or comic, a raga should illustrate. He could vividly feel, see and sympathise with the various sentiments of a raga—despondency, timidity, heroism, anger, tenderness, contentment, joy and sorrow and let the tone of his voice and the play of his countenance be in keeping with those sentiments. In fact, he could be what he sang.

The Ragamalika over, he jumped into the dark mine of *Panthuvarali*, traversed the whole cavity with a self propelling light and amazed the wondering andience with a rate set of flawless diamonds of *sangathis* placed before them. Then he commenced a pallavi—*Chandana Charchita Nialkalebra*—in his usually slow measure, the first of the six degrees. None knew where he began or where he ended. It was a labyrinthean web that he wove. It seemed a vast forest of lovely shades and dark shadows which none but a trained hunter could enter and leave, without missing the track. As, however, Marar quickened the degree, the hearers forgot they were on the earth. Some went in trance and some went to dance. Some felt transported to the region of mystery and others perceived the moral value of their lives raised Some again felt the thrill of battle and others thought they were initiated into the sereness of meditation. While thus their ears fed on their ambrosia, their tears flowed down their cheeks.

Thiagaraja, visibly moved, exclaimed; "Beautiful, beautiful! Your silvery music is as charming and fascinating as my golden Rama. Vadivelu misled me by saying you knew only 'a little to sing' Now it is clear you are a Master of Music. Yes, you are a Master greater than even Lord Govinda. I therefore call you, not Govinda Marar, but Govinda *Swami*."

"I would rather be Govinda *Das*," wa Marar's humble reply.

Anyhow Govinda Marar thenceforward went by the name of Govindaswami; and his Varnas were, as they are even to-day, called "Govindaswami Varnams." Thiagaraja's pride melted before the fire of Govindaswami's music; and a song of humility at once issued out from him, much in the style of Govindaswami's Varnas. This was *Entharo mahanubhavulu:* "Many indeed are the great men of the world; to them all I pay my respects,"

Govindaswami, on his part, felt that, with this one color, Thiagaraja drew such a marvellously beautiful picture as to throw his own, so elaborately done, quite into the shade. Not long after, our saint composed four more songs in the wake of *Entharo mahanubhavulu* in Nata, Gowla, Arabi and Varali, to which a common name of *Pancharatna* was given.

These 'Pancharatnas,' be it noted, were composed after the model of Govindaswami Varnas. But Thiagaraja's natural disinclination to compose Varnas or Ragamalikas which, he thought, formed the special work of a Text-Book Writer, made those *Pancharatnas* merely fragmentary, from the Varnapoint of view. *Koluvayunnade* in Bhairavi, however, keeps the Varna-spirit, though a Krithi in form.

CHAPTER XII

HIS SIGNAL SERVICE.

THE signal service the saint rendered for the music-world may be said to be five-fold:—

1. He surveyed, with a comprehensive view, all that science had till his time produced; measured the talents and resources of some of the more important preceding artists[4]; and focussed all their rays in his novel Krithis.

2. As a necessary corollary, he introduced, for the first time in the history of Indian Music, the system of developing "sangathis" or music-phrases.

3. Incidentally, he extricated music from the tyrannical grip of words.

4. He emphasised the principle that prose suits music far better than poetry.

---

4. For a List of Musicians and Scientists to whom he elt indebted, see his krithi in Mayamalavagowla, *Vidulakumrokkade*, wherein he referred to Kamala, Gowri, Vagiswari, Brahma, Vishnu, Siva, Narada, Amaresa, Bharata, Kasyapa, Chandisa, Anjaneya, Gajamukha, Markendeya, Agasthya, Nandi, and even Sharangadev author of *Sangitharatnakara*. Mr. Thirumalayya Naidu's view that Thiagaraja "inherited nothing from those who preceded him," is obviously incorrect.

5. He crystallized the *apurva* or rare ragas into so many krithis, but for which those 'apurva' ragas would have long ago vanished into airy nothing.

These five points we shall consider in detail.

A bird's eye-view of Indian Music from the pre-historic time down to Thiagaraja's day shows that the growth of music could be brought under four main stages, viz, Talking, Speech, Emotional Speech and Recitative Music. Prose talk, Prose chant, Verse chant and Lyrical Song were never distinct from, but ever tended to shade with, one another. Nay, human speech passed into all the four states between which the only line of demarcation was the degree of emotion.

In war, some set phrases were singled out from common talk ; in funerals, some other phrases rose into prominence ; in hunting, the hunters' emotion took a poetical from which they chanted ; in story-telling a meaningless chorus asserted itself. From these small beginnings, there emerged a distinct stage when orations or highly emotional speeches came to be delivered. These orations will be found, on careful examination, to have grown out of simple talking, even which has a rise and fall in pitch. They distinguish by intonation questions from answers; touch emphatic words with a peculiar accent; and form thus a phase of music which may be roughly written down in notes. The more emotional a language is, the more musical it becomes. Compare for instance, the emotional language of Andradesa with the monotonous one of the Nilgri Hills. If even simple talking has its own rise and fall in pitch, the emotional speech of a trained orator is invariably accompanied by exalted tones and cadences. "Just as," observed Herbert Spencer, "from the orations expressed in the metaphorical and allegorical style natural to them there sprang epic poetry out of which lyric poetry was afterwards developed; so, from the exalted tones and cadences in which orations were delivered, there came the chant or Recitative Music from which Lyrical Music has since grown up. The parallelism lies not only in genesis but also in results. For, lyrical poetry differs from epic poetry just as lyrical music differs from recitative music. Each still further intensifies the natural language of the emotions. Lyrical poetry is more metaphorical, hyperbolic, more elliptical and adds the rhythm of lines to the rhythm of feet. So lyrical music is louder, more sonorous, more extreme in its intervals, and adds the rhythm of phrases to the rhythm of bars. And the known fact that out of epic poetry the stronger passions develop lyrical poetry, strengthens the inference that they similarly developed lyrical music out of recitative."

This theory of Herbert Spencer had been already anticipated by our ancestors, inasmuch as they classified Music into two broad divisions, *Margi* and *Desi*. Text-Book Writers have defined 'Margi' to be what was *sought for* by Brahma and practised by Bharata; and 'Desi' to be what varies according to the tastes of the people of various *countries*, tending to the gratification of the sense of hearing. Again, Margi is said to be *Bhavabhanjana* or Destroyer of Birth; and Desi', *Janaranjana* or that which pleases the people. The former represents the old style and the latter, the new style. But wherein lies the vital point of difference between the two styles? Mathanga answers; "Margi is *Nibadha* or set in and bound by words; while Desi is *Anibadha* or free from the slavery of words." This exactly is the difference between Herbert Spencer's "Recitative and Lyrical" music. Hence Margi is Recitative music; and Desi, Lyrical Music.

Samaganam is *Margi* or Recitative music in a crude form. The whole of the Ramayana was sung by Kusa and Lava so excellently that all the ascetics that heard the music were struck with wonder, and, with eyes flooded with tears, exclaimed: "Ah! What charming music! What sweet verses!" What kind of music could it have been but the same Margi or Recitative Music, though in a refined form? Has the reader at any time heard Ramayana Sastris expounding to their eager audience the whole poem, or a part thereof, in a subdued chant? That again, is Recitative Music. Has he noted that Harikatha performers first make speeches, then slowly take their audience to vrithas (verses) and then to avatharikas (Introductories), which could imperceptibly develop into full-fledged songs? That exactly was the way in which music grew stage by stage.

As time went on, Recitative Music fell into two divisions, viz.

(1) Recitative Music, pure and simple, which took the name of Vrithas; and

(2) Kirthanas,[1] the function of which was either a narration or prayer—

---

1. Kirthanas, like Vrithas, are set in or bound by words and lend themselves to prayer. Hence they came under Margi or Bhavabhanjana or Recitative Music.

A commingling of these two divisions marked a distinct epoch in the history of Indian music; and Arunachala Kavi'sı *Rama Natakam*, consisting, as it does, of Vrithas and Kirthanas, fully represented that epoch. It was published in 1772, when Thiagaraja was a boy of 13 years.

Side by side with this development, the composition of Varnas, Ragamalikas, and Swarajits was in its fullest swing. Text-Book Writers, like Venkatamakhi, composed Lakshanagithas Varnas and their paraphernalia to illustrate the principles they discussed in their text-books. Hence this special species of composition was primarily intended to help the learners to understand the principles enunciated in texts but never to be displayed before an audience. Later on, sahithyas (wording) were added to the swaras, with the result that both the swaras and sahithyas became a matter for display. Special pains were then taken to see that the letters of the *sahithyas* were, as much as possible, the very letters of the swaras, as for example. *

*** For an explanation of signs employed in the figures that follow, see my *Sargam Notation*.**

●	I	I	I	●	○	●	○
त—क	त—क	त—क	त—क	त—क	त—क	त—क	त—क
पमा ऽप	धप माऽ	गारि गमा	ऽग मस	मा पध	पमा ऽग	गमा ऽग	मप पध
Uma pa	thiku ma	rani gama	gama sa	ma srutha	vinma na	gama ga	mara hitha

This habit finally led the South Indian musicians to their peculiar *Swarajnanam*. To what kind of music do the Varnas and Ragamalikas belong? Doubtless, they belong to Recitative Music, for they are no better than Kirthanas, with an additional burden of swaras. Further, they are Nibadha and, lending themselves, as they do, to prayer, come under the category of Recitative music.

We will not be far from being true, if we infer that, prior to Thiagaraja, South Indian Music was in the Recitative stage and that it fell to the lot of Thiagaraja to carry it on to the next stage of

Lyrical Music. Indeed Thiagaraja focussed in his novel krithis all the rays of music previously found scattered among Vrithas, Kirthanas and Varnas. While narration or prayer formed the uniform subject-matter of these three, each of them had a special, and even distinct, feature to mark out from others. The development of sangathis was the special feature of Vrithas; the control of thala, of Kirthanas; and the swara vinyas, of Varnas. Thiagaraja happily blended all these three features in his krithis and presented to the world an entirely new and fascinating species of composition.

Though he was not inclined to compose Varnas and Ragamalikas, as they formed the special work of a Text-Book Writer, which he never was, he made a few of his krithis look like, and even savour of, them. Some adopted only their spirit ; such as *Koluvaiyunnade* in Bhairavi ; and some kept their form, though fragmentary, such as, his *Panchratnas.*

The way in which the various sangathis or music-phrases succeed one another in his Krithis is highly artistic and felicitous. The first sangathi is a very simple melody ; the next is a little elaborate; the next is still more elaborate; and so on, until the last brilliant sangathi presents, in the compass of the same *avarth* or time-limit as the first sangathi, the maximum of rythmic liveliness and melodic fulness. All the sangathis glide into one another so easily and so gracefully that they seem to be natural evolutions and involutions of one another. Thiagaraja will ever be remembered for this striking innovation which has doubtless enriched music to a most astonishing degree.

We shall take a Krithi say, *Niravadhisukhada* and illustrate the development of sangathis we have been discussing.

HEADING

Mela Harikamboji	Janyaraga	—— Ravichandrika.
	Thala	—— Adi.
	Kâla	—— Madhyma.
	Gathi	—— Chathusra.

Arohana—स—रि—ग—म—ध—नि—ध—सं
2 2 1 2 1 2

Avarohana —सं—नि—ध—म—ग—रि—स
1 2 1 2 2

SONG.

Pallavi.

Niravadhi Sukhada, Nirmalarupa.
Nirjithamunishapa.

Anupallavi.

Sharadhibandhana, Nathasankrandana,
Shankarâdigiyamana Sadhumanasa Susadana

Charanam.

Mamava Maragatha Maninibha deha
Srimanilola Srithajanapala
Bhimaparakrama, bhimakararchitha
Thamasarajasamanavadoora Thiagaraja
vinuthacharana.

● त—क	। त—क	। त—क	। त—क	● त—क	○ त—क	● त—क	○ त—क
PALLAVI.							
* स रि	ग म	रि स	रिग मग	रिग मग	रि ग	री ■	गारि सधृ
Ni ra	Va dhi	su kha	dha-——	ni-——	rma la	ru ,,	pa——
,, ,,	,, ,,	,, ,,	मग मध	धनि धम	ग म	,, ,,	,, ,,
,, ,,	,, ,,	,, ,,	dha——	ni——	rma la	,, ,,	,, ,,
,, ,,	,, ,,	,, ,,	,, ,,	,, ,,	पध सां	निध म	मग रिग
,, ;;	,, ,,	,, ,,	,, ,,	,, ,,	rma la	ru——	pa——

●	I	I	I	●	○	●	○
त—क	त—क	त—क	त—क	त—क	त—क	त—क	त—क
,, ,,	,, ,,	,, ,,	,, ,,	,, ,,	मध धसं	,, मग	,, ,,
,, ,,	,, ,,	,, ,,	,, ,,	,, ,,	ma la	,, ——	,, ,,
,, ,,	,, ,,	,, ,,	गम डनी	धम धमी	धध सां	निध मगा	डग रिग
,, ,,	,, ,,	,, ,,	dha——	ni——	rma la	ru——	pa——
,, री	डग ,,	,, ,,	रिग मा	धनि धा	संरिं गां	मग गरि	सां ड
,, ra	va ,,	,, ,,	dha——	ni——	rima la	——	pa——

सनि	निध	षध	सां	निध	म	मग	गरि	सा	ह	द	ध	रिग	मग	गरि	सं
ni——		rji	tha	mu	ni	Sha-——		pa———		———		———		———	
स	रि	ग	म	रिम	म	रिग	मग	रि	ह	घ	ह	सा	ह	ह	ह
Ni	ra	va	dhi	Su	ka	da ——		———		———		———		———	

ANUPALLAVI.

+	पसां		डसं	सं	संरि	धा	डध	सां	ह	रिंग	मंग	रि	ह	मंगं	गंरि	सां
	Shara		—dhi	ba	———		nda	na	—na—		tha	—san	—Kran		da	—na
	,,	,,	,,	,,	,,	,,	,,	,,	,,	रि'रि"	रि॰	ह	ह	स'रि	गंरि	रि॰
	,,	,,	,,	,,	,,	,,	,,	,,	,,	natha	san-——		——Kran		da	na

●	|	|	|	●	○	●	○
त—क	त—क	त—क	त—क	त—क	त—क	त—क	त—क
स'री हसं	धसां हनी	धनी धम	धनी धसं	संनी निध	धम मग	रिग मग	गरि सध
Shan-ka	ra——di	gi —— ya	ma—-na	Sa—dhu-	ma nasa	su——sa	da——na

CHARANAM.

* रिमा	हम मग	रिग (गसा)	हरि गा	ह मधा	हम मग	रिग मग	गरि म
Ma—	—ma va—	ma·-—ra	—ga tha	— mani	—— niba	de———	———ha
,, धसा	हस स	रिग मग	रिग (गसा)	,, समा	हग म	ध म	ध धा
,, Sri—	ma ni	lo———	—-——la	——sritha	—ja na	pa———	—— ——la

पमां	दस' स	स'नि धा	दव सां	— रि'गं	संगं रीं	द म'ग'	गंरिं सा
Bhi	—ma pa	ra——·——	kra mo	— bhi	ma ka	——ra·-—	rchi tha
,, ,,	,, ,,	,, ,,	,, ,,	,, रिंरिं	री' द	द सरीं	गारे री'
,, ,,	,, ,,	,, ,,	,, ,,	,, bhima	ka——	——ra--—	,, tha
संरि' रिसं	धस' स'नि	धनी धम	धनि ध्रस	सनि निध	धम मग	रिग मग	गरि सध
tha--masa	ra—-jasa	ma·-nava	doo --ra	Thia—ga	ra-—— ja	nu—-tha	chara na

CHAPTER XIII

HIS STYLE AND DICTION.

COMPOSERS prior to Thiagaraja, and indeed his own contemporaries, were inclined to give in a song greater predominance to words than to tune. There was no attempt—if at all, a feeble attempt—at variation of music-phrases till our saint's time. Let me not be misunderstood that I altogether condemn the system of giving more importance to words than to tune. I know such a system has its own function to perform, viz., describing a scene or narrating a story or even weaving a prayer; as, for instance, the well-known *Rama Natakam* of Arunachala Kavi who lived from 1712 to 1779, or the recently published[1] *Skanda Purana Kirthanas* of Kavi Kunjara Bharathi, who lived from 1812 to 1897. But I must, in duty bound, tell my reader that description or narra-

---

1. By Mr. N. Kotiswara Iyer, B. A., Kavi Kunjura's daughter's son and himself a Tamil Scholar and Musician who has composed Kirthanas in some of the 40 Extra-ordinary Ragas.

tion or even prayer belongs to the province more of poetry than of music and leads to the recitative, rather than the lyrical, music. It was the unique glory and privilege of Thiagaraja to have slowly and steadily rescued musical compositions from the tyrannical grip of words and to have recognised that music also has a body to kick and a soul to save; that the words of a song form a mere body or flower, whereof the tune is the soul or the smell, as the case may be; that the song really begins where words end; that the true function of music is the presentation of the highest attainable perfection of unalloyed beauty in sound: and its words are but a mnemonic aid thereto ; and that, to use a figure, music is a Queen, not a Handmaid, reigning supreme over the whole region of her songs, the words whereof must merely act the part of her loyal subjects.

If we take two compositions, one of Arunachala Kavi and the other of Thiagaraja and place them in juxtaposition we shall find that in the former there is no scope for sangathi, while in the latter every letter of the word *Najivadhara* is followed by an interval which gives full scope for the development of music-phrases, as for instance :—

Author	● त—क	| त—क	| त—क	| त—क	● त—क	○ त—क	● त—क	○ त—क
Arunachala Kavi	पध सां	S संमि	निध धप	मग रिग	मा S	S S	मग मा	निध पम
	Idu ko	—— in—	da yo	jana sa	mi ——	——	Hanu man	nan: ruka
	सम गम	पप पम	मनि धनि	संसं संसं	निसं मंगं	गंरिं रिसं	संनि निध	धप पम
	Uda kiren	Indra githa	pada kiren	ava nanam	vada kiren	aiyo diyil	puda kiren	adhi kenn
Thiagaraja	पा S	S S	धप मग	रिस रिगमग	रिगाSरि सा	ससरिस सनिनिध	सा S	गरि गा
	Na——	——	Ji ——	—— va	——	dha ——	——	ra ——

At first, even Thiagaraja could not get out of the groove. It was during this struggling period that he composed Divyanamavali, Bhaktha-Vijayam, Nowkacharithram and other Kirthanas of the first period of his career, all of which are full of words giving almost no room for sangathis. But slowly he felt that his song should put off her adornment of words, since their jingling was calculated to drown God's whispers. He therefore decided that the words in a song ought not to count for more than the song itself. To attain this ideal, he trained himself by composing simple krithis with fewer words than before, such as Giri-raja-sutha, Pahi-rama dootha and other krithis, of the second period of his career.

During this training period, he discovered a secret that music rhythm was quite different from word-rhythm and that an attempt to fit in the former with the latter was something like trying to fit a circle into a square. In other words, good poetry and good music are two independent sovereigns who cannot rule together one and the same territory but must each have an entirely different region, with entirely different laws and regulations to govern it. It is prose that blends beautifully with music and it is prose that Thiagaraja successfully employed in his krithis.

As for his style and diction, Mr. Thirumalayya Naidu observes: "It must be admitted that Thiagaraja is not always very happy in the choice of his language. His diction is neither varied nor copious. His phraseology is commonplace and prosaic. But in Nowkacharithram (an earlier work) he seems to have had a more careful eye on the judicious use of words, though it cannot be said to be free from faults of grammar or idiom. Curiously enough, he sometimes used both Sanskrit and Telugu and, for instance, the pallavi is in Sanskrit and the rest of the krithi is in Telugu, Apart from the sentiments of the songs, they possess little literary merit." Mr. C. R. Srinivasa Iyengar paid a poor compliment to our musician when he wrote: "Thiagaraja used Sanskrit and Telugu but *affected the latter*; while Syama Sastri championed the melodious Telugu." Mr. Lakshmana Pillay was more precise on the point and remarked: "Thiagaraja towers so high in the beauty and magnificence of his music that one is content to overlook the *glaring defects* of compositions in his songs." Mr. K. V. Srinivasa Iyengar admits these defects but piously transfers them to some mischievous interlopers and bad singers that succeeded him. "After the death of St. Thiagaraja," observes Mr. K. V. S. "his compositions have suffered a good deal from the literary point of view." This is, at best, a charitable surmise bordering on hero-worship. The truth is that Thiagaraja never cared, especially in his latter days, to employ poetry of a high literary * order in his songs; and the few songs praised by Pundits like Ramasesha Sastri and Bhashyam Krishna Sastri are our musician's earlier compositions which, like Jayadeva's *Gitagovindam*, come under Recitative Music. In short, Thiagaraja was a music-poet, not a word-poet. The defects of his compositions, if any, looked at from the word-point of view, are nothing compared with the beauty, sublimity, grandeur and magnificence of his heavenly music. All his later songs, that is, of the third period of his career, are all, as it were, dipped in ambrosia, so that when they emerge out of it, the aromatic perfume impregnates the whole atmosphere of music, making you for the time being forget the materials that convey the fragrance.

* Dr. Tagore observes: "Too much literacy is busy with nets and neglects the fishing."

CHAPTER XIV

HIS RAGA AND THALA SYSTEMS

THIAGARAJA'S krithis in apurva-ragas are invariably simpler than those in the *ghana* or ordinary ragas. There are either no *sangathis* therein or, at most, one or two, for the reason that the scope for elaboration is limited therein. Nevertheless, they catch the ear more easily by virtue of their novelty and intensity of feeling which more than compensate the want of extensity or development. Prior to Thiagaraja, the number of ragas used for songs, was very limited. Jayadeva used in his *Gitagovindam* (12th Century) only eleven ragas, viz, (1) Malava (2) Gurjari (3) Vasantha (4) Ramakari (5) Malavagoula (6) Karnata (7) Desakya (8) Desivaradi (9) Gowdakari (10) Bhairavi and (11) Vibhasa, most of which became long ago obsolete. His successors too feared to tread on an unsafe ground. The 264 Ragas of *Sangitharatnakara* (13 th century) were consigned into oblivion. Dissatisfied with Sarangadev's method, Lochanakavi (14th Century) adopted what might be called the Genus-Species system of classifying Ragas. Others followed him with avidity but amended his system, each in his own way, till at last Venkatamakhi set out, in his epoch-making *Chathurdandiprakasika* (1660), his 72 Melas, stereotyped them with a challenge to the music-world that they could neither be decreased nor increased and thus dealt a death-blow to the mania of amendment.

The Raga System that has been prevailing in South India, from 1660, is that of Venkatamakhi. And yet the immediate predecessors of Thiagaraja hesitated to avail themselves fully of the Melakartha Chakra drawn up in *Chathurdandiprakasika.* The Ragas used in *Rama Natakam*, a work that just preceded Thiagaraja's Krithis, were Thodi, Varali, Bhairavi, Kalyani, Saveri, Asaveri, Madhyamavathi, Sankarabharanam, Anandabhairavi, Nilambari, Surati Useni, Atana, Kambodi, and a few others. The melodic sweetness of all other ragas lay unfathomed for a long time. It fell to the lot of Thiagaraja to dive deep into the mysteries of the Raga-development and expound their intricacies in his own characteristic way. He but followed Venkatamakhi's System,[1] selec-

1. The question whether Thiagaraja followed Venkatamakhi or Narada has now lost its importance. Since Swararnavam is lost to us, all the musician's Ragas have been brought into line with Venkatamakhi's System.

ted therefrom so many as 47 Melas and distributed them amongst his 505 krithis.[1] For, it will be seen on analysis that out of 505 Krithis, 95 are in Harikamboji[2]; 85 in Kharaharapriya; 80 in Sankarabharanam; 53 in Hanumathodi; 40 in Mayamalavagowla; 36 in Natabhairavi; 24 in Mechakalyani; 9 in Subhapanthuvarali; 8 in Jalavarali; 7 in Chakravaka; 4 in each of Suryakantha, Kirvani and Sarasangi; 3 in each of Gayakapriya, Jankaredwani, Pavan, Gamanasrama, and Vachaspathi; 2 in each of Vanaspathi, Manavathi, Denuka, Kokilapriya, Vakulabharanam, Gowrimanohari, Vagadiswari, Soolini, Chalanata, Ramapriya, Nithimathi, and Kantha, mani; and only one in each of Ratnangi-Rupavathi, Varunapriya, Mararanjani, Charukesi, Naganandini, Ganjeyabushami, Navanitha, Bhavapriya, Shadvidhamargini, Divyamani, Namanarayani, Kamavardhani, Viswambari, Shanmukhapriya, Simmendramadhyam, and Rishabhapriya.

A clearer understanding of the principle of Thiagaraja's selection of 47 Melas will be possible, only when we study Venkatamakhi's 72 Melas and realise the necessity of dividing them into two Groups—say, Group. A for ordinary Ragas and Group. B for special Ragas.

The following is a Table of Venkatamakhi's 72 Melas:—

---

1. Published by the late Narasimma Bhagavathar.
2. Every Mela mentioned herein means and includes its Janya or Derivative Ragas.

No.	Poorva Melas.	Swaras.	Utthara Melas.	No.
1	Kanakangi	$S\ R_1\ G_1\ M\ P\ D_1\ N_1\ \dot{S}$	Salakam	37
2	Rathnangi	$S\ R_1\ G_1\ M\ P\ D_1\ N_2\ \dot{S}$	Jalarnavam	38
3	Ganamurthi	$S\ R_1\ G_1\ M\ P\ D_1\ N_3\ \dot{S}$	Jalavarali	39
4	Vanaspathi	$S\ R_1\ G_1\ M\ P\ D_2\ N_2\ \dot{S}$	Navanitham	40
5	Manavathi	$S\ R_1\ G_1\ M\ P\ D_2\ N_3\ \dot{S}$	Pavani	41
6	Dhanarupi	$S\ R_1\ G_1\ M\ P\ D_3\ N_3\ \dot{S}$	Raghupriya	42
7	Senavathi	$S\ R_1\ G_2\ M\ P\ D_1\ N_1\ \dot{S}$	Gavambodi	43
8	Hanumathadi	$S\ R_1\ G_2\ M\ P\ D_1\ N_2\ \dot{S}$	Bhavapriya	44
9	Dhenuka	$S\ R_1\ G_2\ M\ P\ D_1\ N_3\ \dot{S}$	Subhapanthuvarali	45
10	Natakapriya	$S\ R_1\ G_2\ M\ P\ D_2\ N_2\ \dot{S}$	Shadvidhamargini	46
11	Kokilapriya	$S\ R_1\ G_2\ M\ P\ D_2\ N_3\ \dot{S}$	Suvarnangi	47
12	Rupavathi	$S\ R_1\ G_2\ M\ P\ D_3\ N_3\ \dot{S}$	Divyamani	48
13	Gayakapriya	$S\ R_1\ G_3\ M\ P\ D_1\ N_1\ \dot{S}$	Dhavalambari	49
14	Vakulabaranam	$S\ R_1\ G_3\ M\ P\ D_1\ N_2\ \dot{S}$	Namanarayani	50
15	Mayamalavagowla	$S\ R_1\ G_3\ M\ P\ D_1\ N_3\ \dot{S}$	Kamavardhani	51
16	Chakravakam	$S\ R_1\ G_3\ M\ P\ D_2\ N_2\ \dot{S}$	Ramapriya	52
17	Suryakantha	$S\ R_1\ G_3\ M\ P\ D_2\ N_3\ \dot{S}$	Gamanasrama	53
18	Hatakambari	$S\ R_1\ G_3\ M\ P\ D_3\ N_3\ \dot{S}$	Viswambari	54

No.	Poorva Melas.	Swaras.	Uthara Melas	No.
19	Jangaradhwani	S R_1 G_2 M P D_1 N_1 Ṡ	Shyamalangi	55
20	Natabhairavi	S R_2 G_2 M P D_1 N_2 Ṡ	Shanmukapriya	56
21	Kiravani	S R_2 G_2 M P D_1 N_3 Ṡ	Simmendramadhyan	57
22	Kharaharapriya	S R_2 G_2 M P D_2 N_2 Ṡ	Hemavathi	58
23	Gowrimanohari	S R_2 G_2 M P D_2 N_3 Ṡ	Dharmavathi	59
24	Varunapriya	S R_2 G_2 M P D_3 N_3 Ṡ	Nitimathi	60
25	Mararanjani	S R_2 G_3 M P D_1 N_1 Ṡ	Kanthamani	61
26	Charukesi	S R_2 G_3 M P D_1 N_2 Ṡ	Rishabapriya	62
27	Sarasangi	S R_2 G_3 M P D_1 N_3 Ṡ	Lathangi	63
28	Harikamboji	S R_2 G_3 M P D_2 N_2 Ṡ	Vachaspathi	64
29	Dhira Sankarabaranam	S R_2 G_3 M P D_2 N_3 Ṡ	Mechakalyani	65
30	Naganandini	S R_2 G_3 M P D_3 N_3 Ṡ	Chithrambari	66
31	Yagapriya	S R_3 G_3 M P D_1 N_1 Ṡ	Sucharitra	67
32	Ragavardani	S R_3 G_3 M P D_1 N_2 Ṡ	Jothiswarupini	68
33	Gangeyabo shani	S R_3 G_3 M P D_1 N_3 Ṡ	Dathuvardhani	69
34	Vagadiswari	S R_3 G_3 M P D_2 N_2 Ṡ	Nasikabooshani	70
35	Soolini	S R_3 G_3 M P D_2 N_3 Ṡ	Kosala	71
36	Chalanata	S R_3 G_3 M P D_3 N_3 Ṡ	Rasikapriya	72

As regards these 72 Melas, Venkatamakhi, who made them, observed:—

येकल्पयिष्यमाणाश्चकल्प्यमानाश्चकल्पिताः ।
अस्मदादिभिरज्ञातायेचशास्त्रैकगोचराः ॥
नानादेशीयरागास्तद्रागसामान्यमेळकाः ।
संग्रहीतुंसमुद्भीताएतेमेळाद्विसप्ततिः ॥

Hence it must be taken that these 72 Melas were intended to include and comprehend all the possible Ragas—that is say, Ragas already made or in the process of making, or even to be made hereafter, current or only found in books, indigenous or foreign. Here is implied an admission that all the 72 Melas are not, and in the nature of things cannot be, current; and the very author of the 72 Melas permitted the *cutting down* of his Chakra by himself setting an example and cutting his own system into 19 Melas, for all practical purposes.

My own view is that the Melakartha Scheme of Venkatamakhi, as it now stands, is what the Rt. Hon'ble Mr. E. S. Montagu said of the Government of India of 1917:—"too wooden, too iron, too inelastic, too antideluvian to be of any use for the modern purposes we have in view." It must therefore be divided into Group. A of 32 ordinary Ragas and Group. B of 40 special Ragas, for the single reason, if not for anything else, that the Ragas of Group. A are based on the well-known 12 Swaras of the All-India system, perhaps of the All World System; while the delicate use of the four special swaras of the Karnatic System viz, Suddha *Ga*, Shadsruthi *Ri*, Suddha *Ni*, and Shadsruthi *Dha*—makes the singing of the 40 special Ragas of Group. B look like cycling on a wire.

Group. A of 32 ordinary Ragas may be tabulated thus:—

Number in Venkatamakhi's Chakra.	Serial Number.	Purva Melas.	Swaras.								Uttara Melas.
8	1	Thodi ...	S	R_1	G_1	M	P	D_1	N_1	Ṡ	Bhavapriya.
9	2	Dhenuka ...	S	R_1	G_1	M	P	D_1	N_2	Ṡ	Subhapanthuvarali.
10	3	Natakapriya ...	S	R_1	G_1	M	P	D_2	N_1	Ṡ	Shadvidamargini
11	4	Kokilapriya ...	S	R_1	G_1	M	P	D_2	N_2	S	Suvarnangi.
14	5	Vakulabaranam ...	S	R_1	G_3	M	P	D_1	N_1	S	Namanarayani.
15	6	Mayamalavagoula.	S	R_1	G_2	M	P	D_1	N_2	Ṡ	Kamavardani.
16	7	Chakravakam ...	S	R_1	G_3	M	P	D_2	N_1	S	Rampriya.
17	8	Suryakantha ...	S	R_1	G_2	M	P	D_2	N_2	Ṡ	Gamanapriya.
20	9	Natabhairavi ...	S	R_2	G_1	M	P	D_1	N_1	Ṡ	Shanmukapriya.
21	10	Kirvani ...	S	R_2	G_1	M	P	D_1	N_2	S	Simmendramadyam.
22	11	Karaharapriya ...	S	R_2	G_1	M	P	D_2	N_1	S	Hemavathi.
23	12	Gowrimanohari ...	S	R_2	G_1	M	P	D_2	N_2	Ṡ	Dharmavathi.
26	13	Charukesi ...	S	R_2	G_2	M	P	D_1	N_1	Ṡ	Rishabapriya.
27	14	Sarasangi ...	S	R_2	G_2	M	P	D_1	N_2	Ṡ	Lathangi.
28	15	Harikamboji ...	S	R_2	G_2	M	P	D_2	N_1	Ṡ	Vachaspathi.
29	16	Sankarabaranam ...	S	R_2	G_2	M	P	D_2	N_2	Ṡ	Mechakalyani.

The remaining 40 Ragas come under Group. B.

Full well did Thiagaraja know the difference in point of difficulty between the ragas of Groups A and B; and hence, out of 47 Melas that he selected, 31 were taken from Group. A, while only 16 from Group B. And again out of his 505 songs, so many as 485 were placed in Group. A; while only 20 were relegated to Group. B.

It is interesting to note that our saint delighted more in Poorvamela Ragas than in Utharamela ones, for 439 krithis are in the former, while only 66 krithis are in the latter.

Except the first few ragas, all others are 'apurva' ragas which, as said above, would have got into oblivion, if Thiagaraja had not handled them in a felicitous way. On the whole, the number of Ragas, both janakas and janyas, used by Thiagaraja, comes up to a little more than 200.

As for Thalas, the Karnatic system mentions 7 Thalas, each of which ramifies into 5 Jathis.

Hence the 35 main Thalas of the South Indian Music may be tabulated thus:—

Number.	Thalas	Jathis				
		Chathusra	Thisra	Khanda	Misra	Sankirna
1	Eka ...	4	3	5	7	9
2	Rupaka ...	6	5	7	9	11
3	Jampa ...	7	6	8	10	12
4	Thriputa ...	8	7	9	11	13
5	Ata ...	12	10	14	18	22
6	Matya ..	10	8	12	16	20
7	Dhruva ...	14	11	17	23	29

But Thiagaraja ignored this elaborate scheme of thalas and confined himself only to five thalas, viz,

(1). Chathusra Thriputa—E g. *Enthavedukonthu.*)

(2). Thisra Thriputa—(e g. *Endudakinado.*)

(3). Chathusra Rupaka—(e g. *Sujana Jivana.*)

(4). Thisra Rupaka—(e. g. *Nivadane kana.*)

and.

(5). Misra Jampa—(e g. *Dayaleni brcdukemi*)

More than half of his krithis are found in Thala No. 1; and the rest is divided between Thalas Nos. 2 and 3, while only a few are relegated to Thalas Nos. 4 and 5.

CHAPTER—XV

HIS INSTRUMENTS OF MUSIC

THIAGARAJA'S *Kaddanuvariki* and *Koluvamare gada* emphasise, alike, the importance of the time honored, Thambura, for the purpose of drone—and not of the now—unfortunately—prevailing Harmonium ', Whoever advocates," observed Mr. Clements[1] of the Bombay Civil Service, "the use of tempered instruments—such as the Harmonium doubtless is quite unaware of their utter inadequacy to give any idea of Indian intonation." Another careful European student of Indian Music, Mr. Fox Strangways, was struck with the strange ways, wherein the Indians admired and adopted the western instrument and indignantly remarked: [2]

" If the rulers of Native States realised what a death-blow they were dealing at their own art by supporting or even allowing a brass band; if the clerk in a Government Office understood the

---

1. In his " Introduction to the study of Indian Music."
2. In his " Music of Hindustan."

indignity he was putting on a song by buying the gramaphone which grinds it out to him after his day's labour; if the Muhammadan (and for that matter even the Karnatic) singer knew that the Harmonium with which he accompanies was ruining the chief asset, his musical ear; if the girl who learns the pianoforte could see that all the progress she made was a sure step towards her own denationalisation—they would pause before they laid such sacrilegious hands on Saraswathi."

If, in spite of the European's warning against the European Harmonium and of the Indian's emphasis on the importance of the Indian Thambura, our people still persist in the use of the vicous monster of the tempered instrument, the reason is to be sought for, in the never-untrue lines of Alexander Pope—

"Vice is a monster of so frightful mien,
As, to be hated, needs but to be seen;
Yet seen too oft, familiar with her face,
We first endure, then pity, then embrace."

Vina and *Venu* have been the time-honored accompanying Instruments of music in India, Narada being noted for the former and Sri Krishna

---

* For, a monster the Harmonium *is*, inasmuch as it gloats on suffocating the Indian intonation.

for the latter. Our saint recognised the utility of both of them in his *Samsarulaithenememi* of Saveri Raga and *Prananathabirana* of Soolini Raga respectively.

Violin, an undoubtedly foreign instrument, was introduced into Madras and handled by men like Vadivelu. But it never rose into popularity during the time of Thiagaraja who, therefore, made no mention of it in his works. Be it remembered, by the way, that the present importance of Violin in South India is due, in no small degree, to that master-mind, Thirukodikaval Krishnier. In North India, its use is even now very rare.

As for percussion-instrument, the krithi *Sogasuga Mridanga Thalamu* in Sriranjani shows that Thiagaraja recognised Mridangam and (mark !) Mridangam alone ; but not Kanjra, Dolak, Ghata, and a host of other antiquated instruments. The history of musical instruments reveals that, of all percussion-instruments, Mridangam is the highest and latest product. To use therefore in a musical performance all the out-of-date and superseded instruments, side by side with, or (what is worse !) sometimes even without Mridangam, is as absurd and ridiculous as a Master of Arts using after his name all his previous and superseded titles, such as, "Matriculate, F. A., B. A., and M. A." Again, the same krithi makes a telling suggestion that the singer, like a master, should ever come to the front and play the role of "Sokkaseyu Dhirudu," while the instrumentalist, like a servant, should remain in the background and give the singer the needed relief ; and that, if the order is reversed, much the same chaos and confusion will ensue in the region of music, as we witness in the region of politics, consequent upon the servant of the Executive Council lording it over the master of the Legislative Council and reducing it to a despicably "Glorified Debating Society."

CHAPTER XVI

HIS CONTEMPORARIES

OF Thiagaraja's contemporaries, reference has already been made to Swathi Thirunal, Vadivelu and Govinda Marar, as well as to the satellites that moved around the Maharaja of Travancore, his sister Rukmini Bai, and his Dewan Subba Row. I shall now enter into a few more details and try to present a full picture of the Music-World, in South India, during the time of Thiagaraja.

Swathi Thirunal (1829 to 1847) was doubtless the central figure of the picture. He was the royal composer and poet of Travancore. His Varnas, Kirthanas, Padas, and Thillanas were marvellously beautiful. Two of his kirthanas epitomised the whole of the *Ramanayam* and the *Bhagavatham*, while another popularised the Sthala Mahatmyam of Trivandrum. A peculiar feature of his compositions was the free use in them of the very swara letters to which no less a personage than Visakam Thirunal testified: "the swara letters are in themselves meaningless, but Swathi Thirunal most adroitly introduced them in several of his compositions and made them meaningful." When one of his court-musicians, Parameswara Bhagavathar sang an air in swaras most elaborately woven, it is said that Swathi Thirunal instantaneously followed it up with apt words to suit the swara letters.

Next in rank to His Highness, was Iravi Varman Thambi (1783 to 1853), the finish and beauty of whose musical compositions were hardly inferior to those of the Maharaja. They used to show each other their respective compositions and set much value on each other's appreciation.

Another contemporary composer of much repute was Sivarama Gurudasa better known as Kshirabdhi Sastri, a native of Tinnevelly. His songs were pervaded by a spirit of Vedantism and were calculated to popularise the Vedantic truths. Swathi Thirunal and his successor held him in high esteem

Four brothers, orginally of Tanjore, namely, Vadivelu, Sivanandam, Chinayya, Ponnayya, ornamented the court of Swathi Thirunal as experts of violin, drum, dance and Varnam-composition respectively. Of these, Vadivelu was the first brother and was popularly known as Nattuvan Vadivelu. He was dark, lean and squint with one eye; and his voice was powerfully melodious. A Thillana composed by him in praise of the Maharaja is still extant; and his only Varna showed an exuberance of the imagination characteristic of a born musician. Swathi Thirunal and Vadivelu jointly composed a Varna in Kapi that bore thereon the influence of Thiagaraja. Unlike other Varnas, its Pallavi was decked with beautiful variations that bespoke some acquaintance with our musician-saint. Anyhow Vadivelu was known more as a violinist than a vocalist. It was he that, for the first time, introduced violin into South India in general and into Travancore in particular. Mr. Vedadrisadasa Mudaliar attended several musical entertainments at Dewan Subba Row's quarters wherein Vadivelu took part; and in all of them, Mr. Mudaliar noted him only as a violinist. His mission to invite Thiagaraja to the court of Swathi Thirunal and his presence during the interview between Thiagaraja and Govinda Marar have already been referred to.

Of the other three brothers, Ponnayya alone deserves special mention; for he was a gifted composer. His Kambodi Varna *Sarasijanabha*, is even now very popular throughout the Presidency of Madras.

But perhaps the greatest musicians of Travancore that adorned the court of Swathi Thirunal were Govinda Marar and Parameswara Bhagavathar. We have already known Marar; and it is Parameswara Bhagavathar that must now be studied.

It is said that Parameswara Bhagavathar lived to the advanced age of 77 and saw the beginning and culmination of Travancore Music of the 19th century; for, he lived from 1815 to 1892. He was a Brahmin of Palghat, and of Brihacharaman sect. When he visited Trivandrum in 1833 to witness a festival, he was heard by Swathi Thirunal to sing a song in the temple and was forthwith retained in the services of the Maharaja and, later on, appointed as the chief among the court-musicians. He was the Guru of Coimbatore Raghavier. His music was of a high order and in the matter of singing *thanam* he stood unrivalled. Indeed he was responsible for broadcasting the Karnatic Music and popularising Thiagaraja's krithis throughout the state of Travancore.

Meruswami was a Mahratta Brahmin of Tanjore and got into the services of Swathi

Thirunal as a Katha-Performer and gave in the palace of Trivandrum periodical *kalakshepams* in the course of which he made ample use of Thiagaraja's krithis.

Outside Travancore, there were Saraboji (Raja of Tanjore), Thodi Sitaramier, Venkatramier, Kothandaramier, Arunachala Kavi, Ramaswami Dikshithar, Muthuswami Dikshithar, and Syama Sastri, all of whom were undoubted contemporaries of Thiagaraja.

Saraboji was a great lover of music; and the story of his inviting Thiagaraja to his palace and of the saint's singing, in response, *Nidhisalasukhama*, has already been told.

Sitaramier was a favourite musician in the court of the Raja of Tanjore; and *Thodi* was prefixed to his name, for he could sing *that* Raga in an inimitable manner. Curiously enough, he once mortgaged his *Thodi*, as a security for money borrowed and undertook not to sing that Raga anywhere at any time, till he repaid the loan. When, in a performance given before Saraboji, *Thodi* was missing, the Raja specially asked for it; and the mortgage secret was revealed to him. Forthwith he laughed heartily in appreciation of the money-lender's taste for music, paid up the loan, and redeemed the mortgage. The palace-hall once again reverberated with Sitaramier's *Thodi*. It is said that Thiagaraja used to pay periodical visits to this palace-Vidwan, who was senioı to him in age, and submit to him his new compositions for approval. He had as much admiration for this human Sitaram, as he had for his own divine Sitaram.

Venkatramier and Kothandaramier were two Brahmin musicians of Chattanathapuram near Shiyali; and they made common cause with Arunachala Kavi and gave him tunes for which the Kavi gave the composition in words. *Rama Natakam*, therefore, was really a conjoint work of this Trio; and it represented the music of South India, just prior to the time Thiagaraja.

Another Trio that lived during the time of our saint consisted of Ramaswami Dikshithar (1735-1817). Muthuswami Dikshithar (1775-1835) and Syama Sastri (1763-1827). They were all, alike, Varnam-composers which Thiagaraja was not. Dikshithars and Sastri cared more for style and diction, while Thiagaraja cared more for melody and sangathis. The former's music bordered on recitative, while the latter's music was quite lyrical. The former's beauty vanquished by efforts successively repeated; while the latter's, by a single blow. Mr. A. M. Chinnaswami Mudaliar's conclusion is also the same; for, he writes, in his *Oriental Music.**—"Thiagaraja's krithis please the moment they are heard; most of Muthuswami Dikshithar's have to be studied and heard over and over again before their intrinsic merits can be fully realised."

That such 'vanquishing by a single blow' has been the aim of Thiagaraja is amply borne out by his studied use of the word *Drakṣharasa* (grape juice), as opposed to *Nalikerarasa* (cocoanut juice), in his Sriranjani krithi, *Sogasuga mridanga thalamu.* The readerwill note that,if a person simultaneously purchases grapes and cocoanuts, he can *at once* put the former into his mouth and taste their juice; but, as for the latter, he will have first to remove the fibrous rind; then to break open the shell; and still again to separate the kernel therefrom. In other words, grapes give him *immediate* pleasure; while cocoanuts, only after undergoing a little preliminary difficulty. The Indian philosophers

* Vide Introduction; para 110.

agreed to call whatever gives immediate pleasure—*Drakshara sa*; and whatever gives pleasure only after some preliminary difficulty, 'Nalikerarasa.' In the matter of his krithis, Thiagaraja preferred the former to the latter. Compare, for instance, Dikshithar's *Balagopala* with Thiagaraja's *Koluvyiunnade.*

We need not for this purpose go through the whole compositions. Enough that we glance at the closing portion of each. From the basement of *charanam*, Dikshithar works, like a plodding student, his way up, step by step, to reach the Pallavi; while Thiagaraja, like a genius that he was, solves the problem at a stroke.

CHAPTER XVII

HIS PHILOSOPHY

NOWHERE does Thiagaraja give us any systematic exposition of his philosophy. His songs like Tagore's writings, "form a sigh of the soul rather than a reasoned account of metaphysics." Yet, they do reveal his intellectual and moral creed; and this creed it is which I propose to develop here.

Reference has already been made to Thiagaraja's four periods of career, in connection wherewith, Mr. T. V. Seshagiri Aiyar observed: "All devotees are fanatics at start. The mellowing influence comes from His grace late in life. That is why our ancients attached so much importance to Saguna upasana. It is the road to Nirguna devotion and to Jivan Mukthi itself. Thiagaraja's career is an excellent illustration of this travail of the pious soul. His intolerance showed the acme of his devotion to Sri Rama. He next realised that all devotions lead to the path of salvation. His final discovery was the oneness of many faiths. His songs attest to this gradual unfolding of his spiritual development."

In the first three periods of his career, Thiagaraja exhibited himself more as a pessimist than an optimist and more as a fatalist than an advocate of free-will. His songs, composed during these periods, reveal his pessimistic creed. For instance, his *Rookulu Padivelunna* emphasises Goldsmith's dictum—

> " Man wants but little here below,
> Nor wants that little long. "

His *Kasichethe* enforces the truth of Johnson's couplet—

> " But, scarce observed, the knowing and the bold
> Fall in the gen'ral massacre of gold. "

His *Manavini cinuma* reminds us of Pope's vigorous lines—

> " Go, teach Eternal Wisdom how to rule ;
> Then drop into thyself and be a fool, "

His *Dhyanama Varamaina* has its counterpart in the spirited lines of Milton—

> " The mind is its own place, and in itself
> Can make a Heaven of Hell, a Hell of Heaven."

His *Athade Dhanyudura* recalls to our mind Prior's well-known preaching—

> Who breathes must suffer and who thinks must mourn.
> And he alone is blessed who ne'er was born."

And his *Manasa manasamarthyamemi* proclaims the finality of God's Will and is of a piece with Tagore's memorable line—

"We do what we like: yet we do what He likes."

Be it noted that, during the time of Thiagaraja, pessimistic feeling was a matter of universal experience. The religious and philosophical systems of the Hindus, Buddhists and Jains, like those of the *Toa-ism* & the old or even New Testament, were all pessimistic without an iota of doubt. Thiagaraja could not but reflect the sentiments of his day. "The majority of the people," observed. Mr. Buckle, "adopt the current opinions of the day, make no inquiry and cause no wonder but noiselessly conform to the standard of morals and knowledge common to the country and to the age they live in." To this rule, Thiagaraja was, for the major portion of his life, no exception.

No doubt, at the end, our saint slipped into the Human Philosophy of Bhagavad Gita, so successfully revived by. Dr. Tagore. But, as Prof. Radhakrishnan observed: "Between the stern philosophy of Sankara with its rigorous logic of negation and the ascetic ethics of inaction and the human philosoply of Rabindranath Tagore, it was war to the knife. In the centuries of political depression which preceded Sankara's birth, when India was a prey to external invasions and internal anarchy; Buddhism with its gospel of asceticism made a strong appeal to the people of India, who had by then become weary of existence. According to Buddhism, action is the chief end to be avoided. The highest wisdom consists in withdrawing from the world into the depths of the soul. To the Buddhist, this world is transitory, vile, and miserable ; the flesh is a burden, desire an evil, and personality a prison. The great joy in existence gives place to an ascetic code. As the people were at strife with the world outside, they courted a religion which bade them seek peace inside. As the Greek, in the worst days of his political career, was thrown back on his own resources, finding no happiness in the world outside ; even so the Hindu exchanged his balanced out-look on life for a one side abstract view—an individualism which fights shy of the world with its correlate of 'Maya' developed. An imperfect estimate of the values of the world was the result. Reflection became the sole end of man ; and revolt against the world the means to it. The Indian thought that he should realise freedom by cutting off the encumbrances which made man depend upon the chances of the world and secure peace in the solitary existence of the self. It was Sankara's task to effect a synthesis and make out that Hinduism could satisfy even souls trained in Buddhistic principles. We have in the philosophical synthesis left by Sankara a characteristic attempt to combine the central principles of Buddhism and those of the Vedanta religion in one whole. The anxiety to be loyal as far as possible to both Buddhism and Vedantism appears to be the explanation of much of the inconsistency of Sankara's philosophy,"

It was in this "inconsistency" that Thiagaraja struggled for a long time, till at last he got out of the old groove, transformed himself into an altruist and thus fell in with Dr. Tagore.

How the transformation took place we shall now proceed to study.

One fine August evening at 5 o'clock in 1843, Sulochana Mudaliar, the builder of the Tinnevelly Birdge, met Thiagaraja. Sulochana and his major son, Vedadrisadasa (the future High Court Judge of Travancore) were both on their way from

Madras to Palamcotah. The news of the celebrated meeting of 1838 between Thiagaraja and Govinda Marar, doubtless, lured Sulochana to meet the grand old musician of Thiruvaiyar. The father and son Mudaliars approached Thiagaraja and were duly welcomed, warmly received and richly entertained with the sweet music of the disciples, though not of the master.

The music over, Sulochana broke the silence that prevailed ; and the following interesting conversation took place between him and the famous musician, in which even Vedadrisadasa joined, though at the end.[1]

Sulochana:—My brother, Nalla Thambi, gave me a glowing account of your meeting with Marar—

Thiagaraja (interrupting):-You mean Govindaswami ?

Sulochana:—Y—e—s.

Here, Sulochana sighed heavily, as if he had with him a very sorrowful news and yet feared to communicate it.

---

1. I had the privilege to learn of this meeting directly from Mr. Vedadrisadasa Mudaliar who was present there along with his father.

Thiagaraja:—Why do you then call him *Marar* ? I changed his name from Govinda Marar to Govinda Swami. O! How beautifully he sang! Where is he now ?

Sulochana:—Soon after he left you, he went to Tinnevelly and then to Trivandrum. He told all his friends that it had been his unique fortune and rare privilege to have met you here and that you had overpowered him with your admirable *Entharo mahanubhavulu*. He even sang it to us more than once.

Thiagaraja:—Indeed Govindaswami should have polished my krithi and made it nicer to hear. Is he doing well ?

Sulochana:—Well, Sir ; hale and healthy I found him a few months back at Madras ; and I even wished him god-speed, when he left it, on a pilgrimage, for Benares. But, just a day prior to my departure from Madras, I heard he had reached Pandrapur, where he—d-i-e-d.!

Thiagaraja:—Peace ! Peace ! ! Peace ! ! ! (After a pause,) O ! after all he is a young man and ought not to have died so soon.

Sulochana:—True ; but God has *His* own way of doing things.

Thiagaraja:—Why do you say so ? Wil not God adjust His way according to our earnest prayers.

Sulochana:—I wish He had so adjusted. But my young son, whose ideas have been dipped in the vat of western philosophy, now thrown open to us, has been telling me that prayer has no efficacy in this world, inasmuch as it cannot change or even suspend the divine laws but it can only bring us into conformity with them.

Thiagaraja:—Ah ! I'm sorry I forgot it. My old groove of thought seems to refuse to make room for new sentiments especially at this stage of my life. Now I remember that, sometime ago, a learned Brahmin, who delivered here an interesting and instructive lecture on "Avatars," spoke also of this same philosophy of prayer as having been propounded even in our Shastras.

Vedadrisadasa felt now gratified that his new-cherished idea had its blessings even from the Hindu Shastras and said : "I am very glad to hear that our own philosophy has forestalled the

Western philosophy on this vital point. I am of opinion that mere praise of God's *Sugunas* with an overambition to draw Him towards ourselves but with no record to our credit of any virtuous *deed* or a generous *gift* is tantamount to base blasphemy. O, how I wish for a strong wave of seriousness to sweep through our time-honored fallacies! When we know that God has been ruling the world according to the immutable Law of Karma, what is the fun of praying to Him to hold the Laws of Nature in abeyance to suit the convenience of indulging individuals?"

This fearless remark of the budding youth had, however, a salutary effect on our musician's mind; and he calmly replied: "This new train of thought, happily brought back to my memory, is well worth cogitating upon. I should even like to crystallize that thought in one or two of my krithis."

Happily for us Thiagaraja did crystallize the "new thought" in two of his krithis, viz., Chakravaka song, *Sugunamule* and Vanali song, *Aparadamulanorva*, both of which will be explained later on.

Now, after composing hundreds of krithis and kirthanas of different varieties and teaching them to different sets of pupils; our musician felt, especially when his wife had predeceased him leaving behind a duly married daughter, he had been rather too long in the *Grahasthasrama* life and therefore rightly yearned to become a sanyasi.

At this stage, he sang three krithis, viz, *Idisamayamura*, *Kripajoojutaku* and *Gnanamosagarada*. In the first, he remarked that men had been made sheep to the Yagas of Rogue's Matha and felt very sorry to think of the appalling ignorance under cover of which they, like innocent sheep, licked the hands just raised to shed their blood. In the second, he found that the so-called Prabhus (Lords) were so many time-serving sycophants that would stoop to do the meanest thing and please, for their purposes, even the meanest of men. In the third he prayed for practical wisdom.

Forthwith a new train of thought, perhaps in response to his prayer for 'practical wisdom,' passed through his mind like a flash of lightning. He felt at the eleventh hour, (for he was now 88), he must start again with a clean slate. He called back to memory the words of wisdom that had fallen from the lips of the learned lecturer of 'Avatars as well as the bold words of the budding High Court Judge of Travancore. He thought, now seriously, that, while he prayed and prayed his life away, the world was going on and on in its own usual way and questioned within himself whether he did not, after all, waste his life-time in merely praising God's sugunas or excellent qualities with an over-ambition (literally, evil desire) to draw Him towards himself but with no record to his credit of any virtuous *deed* or a generous *gift*. The history of prayer seemed to him the history of disappointment. "Does man after all know," he seemed to argue "how to pray and what to pray for? Now he desires a thing and fervently prays for it. Let us take that God grants it to him. Soon the thing granted begins to prey upon him and proves his deadly enemy. Down again on his knees he goes and raises his supplicating voice that the evil thing may be taken away from him."

How far Thiagaraja was right in this new way of thinking, we shall now discuss.

It is said that, when the big steamer, the *Titanic*, ran upon an iceberg of the Atlantic Ocean and went down ; all the passengers on board the vessel (men, women and children) cried their utmost to God and sent Him their fervent prayers to save their lives. But the God who had heard Gajendra's cry and immediately run to his rescue, now preserved a grim silence. Why? Because the one was a fiction and the other was a fact. In the former we cooked the dish to our own appetite; while in the latter, Nature cooked it for us in her own way. Again, when the Athenians were defeated by the Lacedemonians both by sea and land, they sent a message to the Oracle of Jupiter, Ammon, to ask the reason why they should sustain so many defeats, in as much as they had erected numberless temples to the Gods, adorned them with costly offerings, instituted therein many a pompous and ceremonious festival, and slain thousands of hecatombs at their altars—as against the Lacedemonians who fell very short of them in all these particulars. The Oracle made a significant reply: "I am better pleased with the prayer[1] of the Lacedomonians than with all the oblations of the Greeks." The philosopher, who told us the story, proceeded to show how the most

1. The Lacedemonians' Prayer is:—"O, God! give us all good things, *so long as we are virtuous.*"

vicious man might be devout, so far as his victims were concerned, and how such a vicious man's offerings would be regarded by God as mean bribes and his petitions as gross blasphemies.

Which prayer, then, would be easily wafted to heaven and willingly accepted by God? In answer to this question, Emerson observed: "Prayer that craves a particular commodity—anything less than good—is vicious; and when it is treated as a means to a private end, it degenerates into meanness and theft. It supposes dualism and not unity in nature and consciousness. As soon as a man is at one with God, he will not beg. He will then see prayer in action." Longfellow sang –

"Trust no Future how'ver pleasant;
Let the dead Past bury its dead;
Act, act[1] in the living Present;
Heart within and God o'erhead"

Appar exclaimed—

"உன்கடன் அடியேனைத்தாங்குதல்;[2]
என்கடன் பணிசெய்துகிடப்பதே. ;

---

1. The poet wrote "Act, act' and not "Pray. pray."

2. Your duty is to support my humble self; ānd mine is to labour and wait.

And Lord Krishna advised—

कर्मण्येवाधिकारस्तेमाफलेषुकदाचन ।

"Your business is with *action* and never with its fruits."

The four answers, quoted above, seem to point to the conclusion that the omnipotence of God is limited by man's destiny, that the Law of Karma is the only working hypothesis in this world, that the doer of good karma need not invoke His mercy at all, which will even otherwise deign to be bestowed upon him automatically and that the doer of bad karma (or for that matter, the nondoer of any karma) expects, whenever he prays for special concessions, that the laws of of nature should be held in abeyance for his own convenience.

What, then, is the efficacy of prayer? To answer this question, we have to postulate, at the very outset, an important premise on which alone we can build a workable theory of prayer, viz.,—

" The Universal Cause
Acts not by partial, but by gen ral laws;
And makes what happiness we justly call,
Subsist not in the good of one, but all.

Herefrom we draw an important inference that—

> "All are but parts of one stupendous whole
> Whose body nature is, and God the soul."

If, then, man proceeds, either in the plenitude of his ignorance or in the puff of his pride, to pray for his own selfish ends; such selfish prayer will, in the light of the above-mentioned premise, look as absurd and ridiculous—

> "As if the foot, ordained the dust to tread:
> Or hand, to toil: aspired to be the head;
> As if the head, the eye or ear, repined
> To serve mere engines to the ruling mind."

Two forms of prayer however, we find commonly prevalent among mankind—one for the prosperity of self and the other for the adversity of non-self. Both are wrong; for, the former proceeds from man's ignorance of "the Universal Cause," while the latter from his perverse and perverted nature. The right form of prayer is one that is invoked for the prosperity of all. Hence Socrates advised Alcibiades to adopt the following characteristic form of prayer—

"O! Jupiter! give us those things which are good for us, whether they are such things as we pray for, or such things as we do not pray for; and remove from us those things which are hurtful, though they are such things as we pray for."

Hence Solomon resolved to submit all his inquiries and anxieties to the Will of the Creator and exclaimed, after a laborious process of reasoning—

'O! God! In my act, may Thy great Will be done!"

Hence finally our own Gayatri refers to the prayer of all for all: "*We* meditate on the adorable light of the Supreme Creator of the Universe. May that light guide *our* intellects in the pursuit of truth."

But does God, it may be contended, need to be reminded by man of His duty? Does not Omniscient Almighty know better than ignorant man what is good for him, how much of it he deserves, and when and under what circumstances it is to be bestowed on him? In other words God's Will will be done, whether or no man prays. Why, then, should you and I pray at all, even for the prosperity of all, inasmuch as God's Will will be done, whether or no we pray?

Two lines of answer may be attempted to this question ; but the second appears to us to be more rational.

Firstly ; Our prayer is not to be interpreted as an ill-timed petition of abject beggars, but a well-timed recognition, by the loyal subjects of the Kingdom of God, of the validity—not to speak of the utility—of the eternal laws enforced there. When a knowing man prays : "Let all men be happy"; it conveys no petition nor even a reminder, to God that he should make all men happy ; but it is tantamount to his recognising the validity of God's eternal law that all men are, or should be made, happy. The more he thus cultivates the habit of so recognising, the more he learns to identify himself with the Universal Law itself ; and the more he becomes at one with God Himself. We may therefore safely state that the efficacy of prayer consists in bringing about man's union with God and in strengthening in the former a habit of recognising the validity of the latter's eternal laws. Prayer, in short, reminds—or is intended to remind—not God of His duty but man of the validity of His eternal law as well as of his duty to recognise it as such. This way of viewing the subject of prayer will, like fire, burn all the dross of selfishness from the mind and make it as pure as sterling gold.

Secondly; the fallacy of the question (viz, why, then, should you and I pray at all, even for the prosperity of all, inasmuch as God's Will will be done, whether or no we pray?) is due to the loose use we make of the word 'Peayer.' *Begging* which indicates man's helplessness, *worshipping* which indicates his sense of gratitude and *praising* which indicates his overflowing love—are all confusedly rolled into one word—Prayer. By all means, worship God and justify your innate dignity of expressing your gratitude to Him for kindness received, whether solicited or not. Again, by all means praise Him, for it is the nature of love to praise and love exults in the repetition of loving words amounting to praise. Does not a lover feel his vocabulary too poor to address his mistress—my dear, my dearest, my darling, my honey, my dove, my love, my life, my all, etc., etc. ? So a real Bhaktha has, for the gratification of his love to coin names for his God in tens, hundreds and even thousands; and that accounts for the existence of 'Sahasranama' and 'Brihatsthothraratnakara.' Telling the beads too, like kissing the mistress, is the result of the repetition—loving Love. Hence, we repeat—praise God. But do not beg Him, for two weighty reasons*:—

(1) In major cases, God's Will will be done, whether or no man begs; and

(2) In minor cases, your own Will will have its sway; and begging, then, is out of place.

It was under the stress of some such pressing thoughts, running counter to Lord Tennyson's—

> "More things are wrought by prayer
> Than this world dreams of,"

that a mighty Krithi issued out from Thiagaraja's soul which was to flow and fertilise the world in the fullness of time and carry with it many a tributary stream of panting human souls, finally to the ocean of the eternal truth, viz, 'Service of Humanity is Worship of God.' This truth had long ago proclaimed itself in Isopanishad—

---

* Mr. Salter. in his *Ethical Religion*, backs me up thus:—"Prayer to the Unknown God involves a double vice;—

(1) first, distrust of the beneficence of that order through which he is already manifested and which holds fast, whether we pray or not; and

(2) second, a despair of our ability to act as proximate causes and to bring about the results we wish ourselves."

"Let man, at work here, wish to live a hundred Aeons." This truth, be it noted, revealed itself in Japan in three striking words, "Patriotism, Loyalty and Charity," and raised that country, as though by a magic wand, to a paramount power in the far East. This self-same truth, be it remembered, will ere long convert the miserable Dependency, into the cheerful Dominions, of India. The unique Krithi suggesting the unique truth forms a sign-post to many a wandering pilgrim and belongs to the fourth and last period of Thiagaraja's career. What is that Krithi?

Here it is:—*Aparadamulanorva*, the meaning of which, in *effect*, is:—"* O! God! This is the proper time for you to forget and forgive me for the great offence I committed by offering prayers

---

* The literal meaning of the Krithi is as follows:— "I (Thiagaraja) have a wavering mind: I've not known your (steady) mind; I've created my own difficulties; yet I complain. Again, inasmuch as you, having, ascertained the merits ane demerits of the world (i. e the people), go on protecting them (in your own pre-arranged way). I composed and sang hundreds of kirthanas in order that you might know to save my individual self alone. (irrespective of others). To excuse me for such heavy or serious offences this is the opportunity. Have mercy."

to you, in season and out of season, in the shape of hundreds of my krithanas. Now I know that you have been, from the very beginning, ruling over and protecting the Universe so beautifully as to drive home to these mortals the homely lesson that God helps those who help themselves, that the best help is that help which engenders and fosters self-help and that men must never be taught to crawl with petitions and prayers for selfish purposes but trained to walk erect and trust in God and *do* the right. I wasted my time with mere personal prayers of the *mampahi* type, as though I were the only living being in this Universe and as though I could unfailingly bind you with my prayers, no matter what the nature of my Karmas may be."

Thiagaraja had time only to think out this idea and crystallize in a krithi, as promised to Vedadrisadasa Mudaliar four years back, but not to develop, much less act up to, it. For, the moment the idea got out of him in the shape of a unique Vanali Krithi, he felt a call from the unknown region, wherefrom no traveller returns. He met, in a nocturnal dream, his dearest Rama who addressed him thus:—"Enough of that one Krithi conveying the

Practical Wisdom you called for. That krithi will act as a seed out of which a mighty tree of wisdom will grow. Your life-mission ends here and I shall grant you Sayujya in ten day's time, within which you will do well to become a Sanyasi." The day dawned; and forthwith the necessary ablutions and ceremonies were gone through. Now Thiagaraja became in fact, as he had all along been in spirit, a SAINT.

It is gratifying to note that Dr. Rabindranath Tagore began from where saint Thiagaraja ended. The former, like Shakespeare, sang the Practices of Life; while the latter, like Dante, confined himself to the Theories thereof. But, unlike Dante, Thiagaraja hinted, though at the end of his life, the Practices of Life also and enabled us to have a glimpse of the ancient Human Philosophy of India which, in the hands of Tagore, is coming more and more into prominence.

Take, for instance, the tenth verse of *Gitanjali*: "Here is thy footstool and there rest thy feet where live the poorest and lowliest and lost." The Hindus are only too familiar with what is called *Padapooja* or Feet-Worship. They generally place before themselves each an idol of

God, made of clay, wood, copper, silver or gold, according to his means, and, having poured water or milk and strewn flowers over its feet—no matter whither their mind roams—feel satisfied that they have done the *Padapooja* required of them. Reader ! this is a huge self-deceit. Thiagaraja only hinted it; but Tagore has drawn our pointed attention to it. His memorable verse, quoted above, drives us to the irresistible conclusion that *Padapooja* is not to be interpreted as meaning only the worship of an idol's feet but figuratively also the worship of "the poorest, and and lowliest and lost," who live in those feet. *Padapooja*, then, really implies the elevation of the depressed (or submerged) classes. But do not the people studiously avoid the uphill-task of elevating the submerged classes but resort to the trick of a comparatively easy-going "chanting and singing and telling of beads" over the feet of an idol ? Hence the immortal Tagore feelingly sang:—

"Leave this chanting and singing and telling of beads ! Whom dost thou worship in this lonely dark corner of a temple with doors all shut ? Open thine eyes and see thy God is not before thee !

"He is there where the tiller is tilling the hard ground and where the pathmaker is breaking stones. He is with them in sun and in shower and his garment is covered with dust. Put off thy holy mantle and, even like him, come down on the dusty soil !

"Deliverance ! Where is this deliverance to be found ? Our master himself has joyfully taken upon him the bonds of creation ; he is bound with us all for ever.

"Come out of thy meditations and leave aside thy flowers and incense ! What harm is there if thy clothes become tattered and stained? Meet him and stand by him in toil and in sweat of thy brow."

This eleventh verse of *Gitanjali*, be it noted, is Thiagaraja's *Aparadamulanorva* writ large.

CHAPTER XVIII

CONCLUSION.

THE ten days promised by Rama were over and Thiagaraja sang his last song *Parithapamukani* in Manohari · "O! Rama! When you were recreating yourself (literally shining), along with matchless Sita, on an excellent golden boat in the midst of the river Sarayu; you (somehow) noted my pitiable condition and addressed me, with a merciful eye, the following words—'In ten day's time, I shall save you.' Have you now forgotten them?' Forthwith our muscian-saint's flame went out and attained Sayujya on Wednesday, January 6, 1847. His body was, with form and formality, buried[1] on the left bank of the Cauvery, a little to the east of Thiruvaiyar; and his graveyard has been visited every year by hundreds of music-lovers on his anniversary day, on which "Thiagaraja's festival!" used to be celebrated more on the religious side. Later on, the religious festival developed into a musical festivity on a par with Handel Festival; and its duration has increased to a week and tends to increase still.

---

1. A Sanyasi's body is not, as a rule burnt, but buried.

Thiagaraja's Samadhi.

Of Bhagavad-Gita it is said that it contains shallows where a child may wade and depths whereunto a giant may fear to plunge. Similarly Thiagaraja's works contain simple and recitative Kirthanas which even a beginner can learn to sing and complex and lyrical Krithis which form the despair even of experts. It is again said of Thiruvalluvar that he is one of the greatest geniuses of the world, though he belongs to South India and wrote for one race. Similarly Thiagaraja is one of the greatest musicians of the world, though he belongs to South India and sang for one race. But taking into consideration the signal service he rendered for the music of India and the fact that, of all musicians, the Festival of Thiagaraja alone the people have taken a fancy to celebrate, year after year, not only at Thiruvaiyar but also in other places; Thiagaraja must be deemed to be the greatest and most popular musician of South India. And the lustre of his name cannot be dimmed by age or impaired by rivalry—any more than the names of Homer, Dante, Milton, Valmiki, Thulasidas or Kalidas, in literature ; *or* of Handel, Haydn, Beethoven, Haridas Swami, Tansen or Gopala Nayak, in music.

APPENDIX.

SARGAM NOTATION.

BY

M. S. RAMASWAMI AIYAR B.A., B.L., L.T.

PART 1.

The notation of European Music is of two kinds, *viz.*, Tonic Solfa and Staff. But that of Indian Music is of only one kind, *viz* Sargam. I venture to name the Indian Notation........... "Sargam Notation"...........because the uniform basis thereof is the Sapthaswaras and the word 'Sargam' is nothing else than an abbreviated form of the first four letters of those Sapthaswaras, *viz.*, Sa—Ri—Ga—Ma.

Notation is to music what alphabet is to language. Ram Das is said to have composed 12,000 songs. Where are they heard now sung ?

They are lost for want of Notation. The Prabandhas of *Gitagovindam* cannot now be sung in the manner of Jayadeva; nor can the masterpieces, collected by Krishnananda Vyas in his *Sangitharagakalpadruma*, be sung in the manner of their authors. "When I", wrote Sir William Jones in his *Musical Moae of the Hindoos*, "read the songs of Jayadeva who has prefixed to each of them names of modes in which it was anciently sung, I had *hopes* of procuring the original music. But the Pundits of the South referred me to those of the West and the Brahmins of the West would have sent me to those of the North. While they, I mean those of Nepal and Kashmir, declared they had no ancient music but imagined that the notes of *Gitagovindam* must exist, if anywhere, in one of of the Southern provinces where the poet was born." Is this not quaint, especially when we know as a historical fact that Jayadeva was born and flourished in Bengal near Dr. Tagore's Shanthinikethan and had nothing to do whatsover with South India? Be that as it may, if Sir W. Jones had been driven from one corner to another, he would have to thank himself for it. For, how could he "hope" to procure the original music of *Gitagovindam*, merely with the help of modes, prefixed to each of its Prabandhas ?* The truth is that there was neither the Notation to record the songs of Jayadeva nor any scientific treatment in his book whereby to teach or even suggest the methods of singing them.

Again, Tansen is said to have electrified his audience with his enrapturing music. Mira Bai is said to have bewitched her audience with her soul-stirring music. Maha Vythinathier, Peria Vythi and Shadkala Govindan are all said to have spell-bound their respective audiences with their inimitable performances. But where are they heard now sung ? They are all lost for want of notation. The remarkable Oratorios of South

---

* Such 'hopes' are entertained even to-day by persons, who, unwilling to take the necessary pains of learning songs at the feet of a Guru, try their best to learn them by the names of raga and thala given over each of them and, as a result, fail. The fact is that the raga and the thala of a song only indicate the broad principles wherein it has to be sung. The information "A lives in Madura" cannot enable you to know in what street, house or part thereof he lives. "Madura" gives you the general direction; but you'll have to make personal inquiries in the town before you can get at A. Similarly "Raga" gives you the general direction ; but you will have to take special pains to learn the particular way of singing the song. So with thala. Has not Thiagaraja composed a lot of songs in the same raga — Thodi ? How will the uniform heading "Thodi" enable you to understand the different songs composed in it, unless you take special pains to learn them ?

India, *viz* (1) Arunachala Kavi's *Rama Natakam*, (2) Gopalakrishna Bharathi's *Nandan Charithram*, (3) Kavi Kunjara's *Skanda Purana Kirthanas*, and (4) Ramaswami Aiyar's *Peria Purana Kirthanas*—are every moment running the risk of getting into oblivion. Why? For want of Notation. The learning process of a pupil takes unduly long time. Why? Again for want of notation. Krithis and Kirthanas are nowadays sung in different ways by different men in different places; and some of them are slowly getting out of use. Why? Once again for want of notation.

Can we drift in this away any longer? Can we, who see unmistakable signs of progress in all other directions, suffer ourselves to be blindfolded in the matter of preserving music for ages? Surely not. We must therefore leave no stone unturned to find out the ways and means whereby to record the superior airs, wheresoever they may come, and transmit them over to our contemporaries and down to our successors to.

Further, it is a historical fact that prior to Writing, Education was necessarily confined to a privileged few and that it began to percolate down to the masses, only after Writing was invented. What Writing is to Language, Notation is to Music. So, for want of proper Notation Indian Music is even to-day, as it has all along been, confined only to a privileged few and has not so much as even touched the vast majority of our Indian brethren. If once the necessity of Music-education for the people at large is realised; Notation will at once, begin to loom more and more into importance.

But to find out a uniform Notation for Indian Music is no easy task. Mr. V, N. Bhatkhande wrote to me on 28th September, 1921 :—" The Girl-Schools of Bombay follow *my* Notation. " Mr. Digambar of Bombay Gandharva Mahavidyalaya speaks of *his* notation. Mr. S. M. Tagore's system centemplates a tnird kind of notation. And Mr. Abdul Rahim's book reveals a fourth kind of notation. In South India, Mr. Subbarama Dikshithar elaborated a fifth kind of notation, while Mr. K. V. Srinivasa Aiyangar employed a sixth kind.

Thus, instead of reaching *Terra Firma*, we have been floundering deeper and deeper in the waves of controversy. Hence, to make the whole country of India recognise and acknowledge one particular kind of notation as a uniform and even *national* one.—is certatnly no smooth sailing.

The foreigners take advantage of our differences and move heaven and earth to foist their Staff Notation into our System. Thus the problem of Notation has been made doubly difficult. In addition to the task of settling our own differences. we have been confronted with another new problem as to whether the Notation for Indian Music should be the European Staff or the Indian Sargam.

Let me first consider the arguments adduced by the advocates of the Staff and dispose of them one by one :—

I. "The Staff Notation is more economical of space than an elaborate Sa—Ri—Ga —Ma—— method of writing."

As against this contention, I submit that in an article, with the spirit of which I fully concur, in the *Hindu*, dated 5th November, 1921, the following remarks were found:—"The Staff music is uneconomical to be used, for it occupies much space and its printing costly." Now, put both the systems of writing a scale in juxtaposition ; and you will see which of the two is more econmical of space.

II. "The Indian Notation has now begun to borrow some of the European signs. See, for instance, Subharama Dikshithar's Notation."

Such borrowing is to be attributed to individual idiosyncracies but certainly not to any in— dispensable necessity. The late Subharama Dikshithar of Ettiapuram borrowed European signs, because he was in the grip of the late Chinnaswami Mudaliar, possessed with Staff mania. But the mere act of borrowing is no argument why the European notation should displace our Sargam Notation altogether. Can a creditor be permitted to kill the debtor, because the later happened to borrow money from the former? Assuming without admitting that Indian music has to borrow some signs from the Staff Notation, the principle that should guide a reformer must be what was chalked out by Lully (1633—1687) the Founder of French music. Seignior Baptist Lully found the French music extremly defective and very often barbarous. However, knowing the genius of the people, the humour of their language and the prejudiced ears he had to deal with, he did not pretend to extirpate the French music and plant the Italian in its stead but only to cultivate and civilise it with innumerable graces and modulations, which he *borrowed* from the Italian. But the question of questions, in this connection, is "Has the Sargam Notation anything to borrow from the Staff Notation ?" I shall presently show it has not.

III. "The Staff Notation has the advantage of a simple 'visual' method of indicating uniformly relative pitch and relative time-value of notes."

The Sargam Notation has an equal advantage of a very simple 'visuo-aural' method of indicating pitch and time. For instance, dots above and below the notes indicate Pitch.

IV. "But the dots are liable to misprint."

So, the semibreves, and minims, crotchets and other varieties of time-value notes are as much liable to be placed on wrong lines and wrong spaces of the stave. Due care and attention in either case will set the matter aright. As for the time-value of the staff-written notes, the scope thereof is very limited from the Indian point of view. Indeed the European and Indian systems of Time-measure are as poles asunder. The Indian Thala is derived from song, while the

European Thala is derived from dance or march. Though both are based on the numbers 2 and 3, the Indian system *adds*, while the Euroean system *multiplies*, in order to form combination of these. While, again, the syllables in a European verse are marked by accent, those in an Indian verse are marked by mathras. Is there any time-signature in the staff to correctly indicate the Sankirna Jathi of Dhruvathal or even the common Kanta Jathi of Atathál, or at any rate, Chowthal of the North Indian System ?

V. "The European Notation has signs to indicate which note is sharp and which note is flat. Much confusion is created in the Indian Notation for want of such signs.

That, in the Sargam Notation, such or similar signs are not made use of in the body of a music-piece while writing it, is at once admitted. But it is submitted that no confusion is created thereby. An average student of Indian Music who is familiar with Venkatamakhi's *Melakarthachakra* knows which notes in a given scale or raga are sharp and which flat. You will have merely to tell him "Melam—8"; and he will at once understand it to be *Hanumathodi* (Hindustani *Bhairavi*) and sound all the notes flatly. Or tell him "Melam—65"; and he will forthwith understand it to be *Mechakalyani* (Hindustani *Yaman*) and sound all the notes sharply. At the head of each music-piece, the names of the Raga and Thala are usually given; just as treble or bass clef, the time-signature and the signs of sharp or flat notes are placed at the beginning of the stave. Nowadays the number of the Melam is also added. These headings alone are more than enough for an Indian music-student to know what sharp or flat notes he has to sound in a given piece. If desirable, the heading of a music-piece, say, *Niravadhisukada* may be as follows:—

Mela. 28 Harikamboji (Hindustani Jinjoti)	}	*Janya Raga*—Ravi Chandrika. *Thala*—Adi. *Kala*—Madhyama.

Arohana :—Sa—Ri_2—Ga_2—Ma_1—Dha_2—Ni_1—Dha_2—Sa
Avarohana :—Sa—Ni_1—Dha_2—Ma_1—Ga_2—Ri_2—Sa

In the body of the music piece, it is enough that mere swara letters are written, inasmuch as the number 1 or 2, indicating respectively the flatness or sharpness of the notes, is correctly inserted in the heading. Be it noted that "Sa" denotes the key-note and "Sa" denotes its octave and that the theory of flat and sharp notes applies only to

Ri—Ga—Ma—Dha—Ni and never to Sa—Pa. Here the European Music would make confusion. We call the first black key in a Harmonium 'Flat Ri'; but the Europeans would call it C Sharp or D Flat. Again we call the second Black key 'Flat Ga'; but the Europeans would call it D Sharp or E flat and so forth. Is not our clear and unambiguous nomenclature decidedly better than the confused one of the Europeans?

VI. The following sixth contention was raised by an educated Indian lady with University honors in a letter writen to me on 26 11-21. To be fair to her, I shall quote her letter at length: "I request you to kindly think over the question of having a Staff Notation, for our music. With the Staff Notation, our music will be studied and appreciated by the Americans, the English, etc.; and there is the chance of Indian Music becoming universal and popular and still Indian. If we wish to be recognised as a nation, we must make others see the greatness and the superiority of all that we possess. How did our great religion, find its way to the United States of America? It was through the common medium—English. At present, the western people make fun of our music; and a few like Mrs.———, who honestly and sincerely wish to know something about our music, are handicapped for want of a common notation. So if we allow music to be written in the Staff Notation. I don't think we need fear of its becoming corrupted. On the other hand, I think it will become rich by absorbing the western music and yet remaining Indian. The time has now come when we should no longer be content with confining ourselves but should go out more and assert to the world that we are a nation."

Which reader of this letter will fail to appreciate the noble sentiment of patriotism and the nobler spirit of independence that run throughout it? Oh! how I wish for many more such learned ladies in our country!

But all the same I fear the writer of the letter, under reference, has not caught my point and all her arguments have therefore overshot the real issue. My contention is, and shall ever be, that the Indians should learn and practise Indian Notation for Indian Music. Her main contention seems to be that the Indian Music should be reduced to the Staff Notation for a twofold purpose, *viz.*, (1) for the benefit of the Europeans and the Americans and (2) for ourselves going out and asserting to the world at large that we are a nation. If so, I hasten to agree with her. But is the Staff necessary—I earnestly ask—for the Indians themselves to study and appreciate Indian Music? The learned lady seems to say 'yes', as inferred from her reference to the Staff as a "common" notation in her letter. Evidently she wishes that the staff should be made a *Common* notation for both the Europeans and the Indians. Here I agree to disagree with her. If a European or American wants to study Valmiki's *Ramanayam* and is yet unwilling or unable to learn Sanskrit; let him by all means read Griffith's translation of the poem and appreciate the orginal author as much as he can. But would he, on that account, be justified in compelling even the Sanskrit knowing people of India to study Griffith and forget their Sanskrit? Similarly, if any European or American wants to study Indian Music and is yet unwilling or unable to learn the Sargam Notation; let him by all means reduce the Indian Music into his own Staff and appreciate it as much as he can. But would he, on that account, be justified in compelling the Indian students to forget their own Sargam Notation in favour of a foreign Staff? True, Swami Vivekananda employed English in the United States of

America to assert the superiority of Indian religion. But did he ever ask the Indians to forget their own Vernaculars in favour of English? Again, the letter speaks of a few Europeans being handicapped for want of a common (*i. e.* Staff) Notation. How many of those "few Europeans," I ask, availed themselves of Mr. Chinnasami Mudaliar's *Oriental Music*, wherein some of Thiagaraja's Krithis had been reduced to the Staff Notation? For aught I know, the Europeans discarded it because there was the *Indian* Music in it; and the Indians equally discarded it, because there was the *Staff* in it. Nor does the learned lady's complaint, *viz.*, "the Western people make fun of our music", frighten us into adopting the Staff. For if the westerners make fun of our music, they really make fun of themselves. For, it is a truism that different races posses different auditory faculties and hence different systems of music came rightly into existence. The Frenchman cannot enjoy the English music, nor can the German enjoy the French music, nor can even the Hindustani Gavayi enjoy the Karnatic music. Hon'ble Sir Charles Turner, Kt. C.I.E., observed in this connection: "the Southern Englishman and the Scotch are within 400 miles of each other; and yet the former cannot honestly enjoy the latter's bagpipe. This difference in taste is due to the difference in the structure of the ear and more to habits and other circumstances of life."* If therefore the westerners make fun of our music, the inference is that the funny element is, not in our music, but in themselves. Reduction of Indian Music into the Staff Notation cannot be a remedy to such "funny" people. They must be prepared to have their tastes changed or modified, before they can approach our music.

VII. As though a seventh contention were raised, a European friend of mine wrote to me on 7-9-1922: "I have now got a native musician, quite ignorant of English, who tells me that it is not imposible for him to reduce all the *Indian* airs into the Staff Notation."

My reply was: "Possible or impossible—that's a different question. Inasmuch as the mother's milk of the Indian (or Sargam) Notation is plentiful for the Indians, why should a foreign Doctor hoarsely cry and unduly praise to the skies the unnecessary Mellin's Food of the Staff Notation?"

---

* *Vide Madras Mail* of 17-11-1884.

VIII "If the Staff Notation is not accepted, why should not the Tonic Solfa Notation be adopted, inasmuch as it has been advocated by no less a person than Abbe Dubois?"

I don't know whether Abbe Dubois ever advocated the Tonic Solfa; but he expressed his over-anxiety to give the whole credit of inventing the music scale to Guy of Arezzo. The French Missionary had, however, to feel surprised to find that the Hindu Music had also the same scale. Here are his own words: "The Hindu Scale bears a striking resemblance to ours, being composed of the *same* number of notes, arranged in the *same* way, as follows:—

Do—Re--Mi—Fa—So—La—Si—Do
Sa—Ri—Ga—Ma—Pa—Dha—Ni—Sa

Are we then to deny the merit of this invention to Guy of Arezzo?" My answer to this last question of the ill formed Missionary is an emphatic "yes." As if to corroborate my answer, W.W. Hunter observed: "The Sapthaswaras passed from India to Persia and thence to Arabia and thence to Europe to which it was introduced by Guido of Arezzo. The European word *Gamut* is derived from the Sanskrit word *Grama*, which means a scale."

IX. As if these eight arguments are insufficient, a ninth argument is adduced with a puff of triumphant air : "The whole of Europe has uniformly adopted the *Staff* Notation; while in India, manifold varieties of notation have been clashing with one another. Is it not, therefore, advisable that India too comes in line with Europe by adopting the *Staff* and thus putting an end to its endless quarrel?"

In the first place, the premises do not warrant the conclusion suggested. But are the premises themselves right? If the cause that enabled Europe to uniformly adopt the *Staff* had existed in India; I have no doubt that our own Sargam Notation would have been, with equal vigour, uniformly adopted. Have, at any time in the annals of the world, the hydra-headed people agreed, of their own accord, on any one point? England could not have become a *Christian* country, if its earlier Sovereigns had not been first converted. Protestantism would have been unheard of, or at least considerably delayed, if the German princes had not, though covertly, supported Luther. Buddhism would not have spread itself, as it did, to East Asia, if Emperor Asoka had not advocated its cause. Similarly, Europe would not have uniformily adopted, as it has done, the Staff Notation; if it had not been forced to do so by the compulsory system of education including Music, that obtained there. Introduce the same compulsory system in our country and soon our Sargam Notation will be the order of the day.

Above all, the Staff Notes are meant more for the eye, while our notes are meant more for the ear. Mr. Hawis, in his *Musical Memoirs*, gives the palm to the ear rather than the eye. If, with a key given, an Indian note Ga is written on a piece of paper, the ear—as soon as the eye is directed to the note—rings within itself the sound peculiar to Ga. But if a European crotchet is written, you cannot at once give its proper sound, even with a help of the keynote given. For some more ceremony has to be performed for it, *viz*, placing it on the correct line of the stave perhaps E, if the given key is middle C. Indeed the European Staff is seven times more unnecessary, more difficult, more cumbrous, more uneconomical and more costly, in addition to its being quite defective from the Indian standpoint.

I am happy to be able to state that quite an array of my friends and others back me up in my position. The Maharaia of Travancore wrote on 29 6 1885 in reply to Captain Day's letter: "Captain Day has to some extent anticipated the difficulties in getting the Hindu airs written out according to the European system of musical notation There are, however, far great difficulties than that of finding a man equally conversant with the two systems. The two systems themselves widely differ in many respects :—

(1) In the Hindu system there are half notes, quarter notes and infinitesimally minute and delicate shades, as in a painting by a master artist ;

(2) The Vocalist or instrumentalist very often glides over a whole gamut or half gamut, backward or forward, in an unbroken easy flow.

(3) In European Music, there is no such thing as Râga, which in the Hindu system is a thing permanently and scientifically established from time immemorial.

Any man possessing the most ordinary knowledge of music will at once recognise the particular Raga, in whatever from of composition (and there are innumerable forms) it is sung to him; and one mis-placed swara will immediately jar in his ears. Indeed with all deference to European Music and appreciation of its soul-stirring effects, I must say that Hindu Music is far more scientific and systematic. In the meanwhile what I have said will in a manner indicate the great inherent difficulties which must present themselves to one who attempts a 'translation' as it were."

Mr. V. N. Bhatkhande of Bombay wrote to me: "I am strongly opposed to making the Staff Notation the sole medium of instruction. My idea is that an Indian notation will go certainly, if not further, at least as far as the Staff Notation, with proper signs and symbols. If, for our gamakas and grace notes, new signs would be necessary even in the Staff Notation, why should we not introduce them in the Indian notation and make it serviceable? An Indian notation will appeal to the Indian mind much more easily. I leave out the question of patriotism and base my opinion on utilitarian grounds." Mr. H. P. Krishna Row of Mysore once wrote a book called "First steps in

Hindu Music in English notation" and by sheer force of experience, changed his opinion and wrote to me (25-9-21): "The Staff Notation is unnecessarily difficult for our music. If we use it, we are likely not to develop our swaragnanam." Mr. P. S. Sundramier of Tanjore wrote: "There is already a notation and the Staff is cumbrous and costly." Mr. Govindasami Pillay of Trichinopoly Mr. Muthiah Bhagavathar of Harikesanalloor and Mr. Mysore Krishniengar—these Vidwans told me they were quite opposed to the Staff Notation being used for Indian Music. S. M. Tagore wrote, in his *Hindu Music*, "The Indian Notation as far as it goes is all that we require. It is simple, convenient and sufficient for all practical purposes. When the Staff of five is still imperfect even in English music, how can it be sufficient for Hindu Music which is rich in Ragas and which abounds in Murchanas, Thalas etc? Every nation that has a music of its own has also its own system of notation for writing it. Whether that system be an advanced one or not, it cannot be correctly expressed in the notation of another nation, however improved and scientific it may be. Anglicised as we have become in many respects, we confess we prefer our national system of notation for our national music. The English system of notation is imperfect and insufficient for the purposes of Hindu Music, for the simple reason that the genius of Hindu music is distinct from that of European Music. In the Staff, we must know what sound is really represented by a note standing upon a certain line or space. The change of keys involves the first line to be C or D or E etc. This indeed is a complicated method. The different systems of music of different nations are not equally progressive; and one uniform notation for all the nations is impossible" Maharaja Sir. P. C. Tagore wrote very recently, in the *Statesman* : "No one who has a thorough knowledge of Hindu Music will venture to deny that it is imposible to accurately represent it by European notation or express it by European instruments. We have already become too denationalised in many things. But for Heaven's sake, let no desecrating hand be laid on Hindu music, which is venerated by orthodox Hindus as being of divine origin."

Last but not least, some of the more responsible Europeans have deliberately arrayed themselves *against* the introduction of the Staff into the Indian System of Music.

Sir W. W. Hunter wrote, in his *Indian Empire*: "It is impossible to adequately represent the Indian system by the European Notation." Sir William Ousely remarked: "Nor are the Hindu airs known to the Europeans from the impossibility of setting them according to the European system of notation. The fact that the Hindus have quarter tones renders it still more difficult to express their music by the European system." Mr. Authur Whitten remarked, in his *Music of the Ancients*, "I have yet to observe that while our (European) system of notation admits of no sound of less than half a tone; the Hindus have quarter tones, thus rendering it most difficult of imitation by the Europeans." Finally, John Curwen, an undoubted European authority on European music, rigorously exposed the fallacy of the position which the adherents of the Staff tenaciously occupied:—"Even in Europe, the Staff Notation presents discouraging difficulties. If a simpler notation be used, the progress will be quicker and far more solid. *The Staff was never designed as a teaching instrument* but was intended to give a picture of the keyboard of pianoforte. The crotchets, quavers, clefs, flats and sharps of the Staff are too abstruse for children and even for men.

A little reflection will show that, although the improvement and wide diffusion of keyboard instruments caused the Staff to settle down into a pictorial representation of blaek and white digitals, this arrangement has no counterpart in the experienee of singers. To them one key is the same as another. This important fact is the basis of Tonic Solfa Notation (which is similar to to the Indian Sa-Ri-Ga-Ma Notation)." Hence Helmholtz, in his *Sensation of Tone*, writes: "Tonic Solfa is the national system of teaching music."

Even in Europe the Staff Notation is not universally accepted. Of 27,330 schools in England and Wales, 21,743 schools teach music by ear only; 1429 by the Staff Notation; 3871 by the Tonic Solfa; 32 by both; and 161 in some other way. Do not these figures speak for themselves?

It would therefore be an unpardonable crime and sin to attempt to thrust it as a compulsory notation into India, where there has been from time immemorial a 'Sargam' Notation from Mount Kailas to Cape Camorin. By all means, join with us in improving our Sargam; but, pray, do not think of throwing it overboard.

"But you have no such thing as Sargam or any Indian Notation at all," thus may retort the puffed advocates of the Staff. So indeed was Mr. R. (a Hindu Musician) taunted some ten years back at Baroda by Mr. F. (a Portuguese musician); and their further conversation which actually took place will be of some interest to the reader.

Mr. R.:—Is not the object of notation to preserve a song and, if need be, to reproduce it?

Mr. F.:—I should think so.

Mr. R.:—Suppose I preserve your song by recording it in my note-book and reproduce it whenever required; will you then grant that we do have our own notation?

Mr. F.:—Surely.

Forthwith Mr. F. sang a snatch and Mr. R. reduced it into his Sargam Notation and even reproduced it. But Mr. F. would not be satisfied and thought that Mr. R. wrote in his note-book some nonsense but correctly reproduced the song by the strength as well as freshness of his memory. They therefore parted for the day but met again next morning at ten. At once Mr. F.

took Mr. R. to a lonely place and challenged him to reproduce, if he could, the song sung the day before. To Mr. F.'s utter disappointment, Mr. R. reproduced the song admirably enough.

The table was now turned. Mr. R. challenged Mr. F. thus :—"Now, Sir, I have reproduced your song and thus proved that we do have our own Indian Notation. I shall sing for you a Hindu air and let me see how and when you will reproduce it.", So saying, Mr. R. sang the well-known Varna-looking Krithi of Thiagaraja's in Bhairavi, viz., *Koluvaiyunnade Kothandapani.* Mr. F. trembled before it, just as Arjuna did before Lord Sri Krishna's Viswaroopa, and confessed : "O! it is all Greek to me : I cannot in the first place conceive your song, much less can I reduce it to my notation."

I wish all the European advocates of the Staff and their Indian allies had been as candid as Mr. F. Their denial of the very existence of our notation even when we are handling it, is nothing different from the proverbial Doctor's certifying that his patient is dead, even though the patient cries : "No, Sir, I am living."

Enough, I believe, has been said to convince you that the system of Notation, most suitable to Indian music, is neither the Staff nor the Tonic Solfa but the Sargam. I must now proceed to place before you what occurs to me the best possible uniform— and I may even say "national" —system of Sargam Notation for the whole of India, which is the main, if not the sole, way to resuscitate our fallen music.

But a preliminary point has first to be settled; for at the very outset we are confronted with the question: "At what stage in a pupil's course of music should Notation be commenced?" Doubtless it is in human nature that as between the thing and its symbol, preference is given to the former rather than to the latter. A hungry man cannot be satisfied with the symbol of bread but wants the bread itself. In education, symbols are needed and employed only when the things they denote are not available or procurable. The true function of Notation, which is but a symbol of music, begins only when the sounding material, the living music teacher, is not available or procurable. Hence the teaching of Notation may be postponed to a later stage, when the chances of the pupils' leaving the school and of being away from the living teacher become greater and greater and may, in fact, be commenced from the First Form, according to my Syllabus. The pupils of the Primary classes who would even otherwise have to encounter the difficulty of mastering the "Notation," so to speak of, of the language (or languages !) they have to learn, need not be encumbered with an additional burden of the music-notation. The method that has to be employed in the earliest stage of a pupil's course of music should what may be called the Imitation or Lip-Ear method. That is the time-honored method too. Further, it is only after the pupils' minds have been saturated with a bit Swaragnanam and Thalagnanam that Notation proper could, with advantage, be commenced. The teaching of Swaras and Thalas should necessarily precede the teaching of Notation.

Is Swara teaching after all nececssary ? Can it not be altogether avoided ? These side issues have of late been causing much anxiety in the music-world of South India, inasmuch as they have emanated from high quarters and attempted to shake the very foundation of Indian Music. I must answer them.

Most managers in schools and most parents in households are obsessed by the idea that every music-piece must at every stage, be capable of—and be ready for—show and display to casual visito s and friends. Surely saralis, alankaras and githas are not adapted for such popular show but are intended to illustrate the principles enunciated in Text-Books on Music. The idea of caring for the visitors' vapoury satisfaction must not be allowed to prevail against substantial and necessarily slow development, especially at the initial stage, of musical knowledge in the pupils, 'The early steps of any art," observed Florence Wickins, "are and must be slow at first; and these beginnings, should on no account be hurried (or avoided). For once the elementary lessons are thoroughly and clearly understood and grasped by the pupil, the rest of the teacher's work is easy." It is those that are impatient of the necessarily slow progress of the early steps of the art who would generally sympathise with the objectors of Swara teaching.

The truth is, just as a man with a mere bone frame is disagreeable, but a man with flesh and blood is agreeable, to look at ; the songs which form the 'flesh and blood' of music are agreeable to hear, but not the swaras as forming the mere boneframe thereof. The on-looker may be satisfied with the sight of the flesh and blood ; but the possessor thereof must take care of his boneframe as well. For, the stronger the boneframe, the healthier the flesh and blood. How can you have a strong boneframe without attending to its growth and development ? And how can you attend to its growth and development without knowing the component parts thereof and the laws of their growth ? In Indian music, the component parts of the boneframe are saralis, alankaras, githas, varnas and other "idioms" of swaras. A learner therefore cannot with impunity dispense with them. Whoever observes "There is no need at all to practise, Jantaswaras and other gymnastic exercises," may as well say that there is no need at all to practise, under the modern system of education, gymnastics and other physical exercises. I would however agree with him, if he should say that the teacher must not make too much of swaras and mistake the means for the end itself. Be it remembered that swara teaching has been, from the time of God Parameswara, the right royal method of music-teaching in India, i nasmuch as Narada said and Thiagaraja repeated in his famous Krithi, "Swararagasudharasa" — that the secrets of *Swararnavam* had been first taught by God Parameswara to Goddess Parvathi. I need hardly tell you that "Swararnavam" was a musical treatise presented by Narada to Thiagaraga. The word Swararnavam literally means 'Ocean of Swaras.' Evidently the book related, as the name indicates, to the illimitable permutations and combinations of Swaras.

I believe you will have, by this time, been convinced of the truth of two important points, *viz.*, (1) The System of Notation, most suitable to Indian Music, is Sargam and nothing else ; and (2) the teaching of Sargam Notation should be preceded by the teaching of Swaras and Thalas.

I shall now proceed to the Notation itself.

PART II.

Each of the 35 main Thalas of South India and of the 25 main Thalas (according to *Abhinavathalamanjari*) of North India—has, on ultimate analysis, three essential parts, *viz.*, clapping, fingering and waving. Note that, when you *clap*, you see the outer part of your hand and, when you *wave*, you see the inner part or palm of it. Is not the palm or inner part of a hand whiter than its outer part ? And is not the outer part blacker than the palm itself ? Hence the Clapping may be represented by a black-sign or New-Moon sign, *viz.*, ● and the Waving by a white sign or Full-Moon sign, *viz.*, ○. The Finger looks like a rod and hence the fingering may be represented by a rod-like sign, *viz.*, I

Now the most popular South Indian Thala is Adi. It has 3 clappings, 3 fingerings and 2 wavings—in all 8 aksharas, which may be represented thus:—

●	I	I	I	●	○	●	○
—Clapping	—Little Finger	—Ring Finger	—Middle Finger	—Clapping	—Waving	—Clapping	—Waving
1 —	2 —	3 —	4 —	5 —	6 —	7 —	8

For every song in the Adi Thala, the following heading is desirable and may, with advantage, be adopted:—

●	I	I	I	●	○	●	○
त-क	त-क	त-क	त-क	त-क	त-क	त-क	त-क

The letters तक (pronounced Tha-ka), in the heading above, denote the mathras or Kalais, the slowness or quickness whereof depends on whether the Kala or time is vilambitha (slow), madhyama (middling) or drutha (quick). "त" denotes one mathra and "क" denotes again one mathra. So one column or bar, consisting of "त-क" denotes two mathras which come to one akshara. The lettters त-क may be written त-त or क-क. It is for convenience of pronunciation that I have given two different letters त-क. But, be it remebered, that each of the two letters denotes one mathra and both together represent one akshara. Again, the lines of the bar are drawn for convenience, sake and have no significance of their own, except the last perpendicular double line which denotes the end of an avartha.

The same principles may be applied to other thalas as well. Take, for instance, Chathusra Roopaka. It consists of 2 clappings, 3 fingerings and only one waving—in all 6 aksharas, which may be represented thus :—

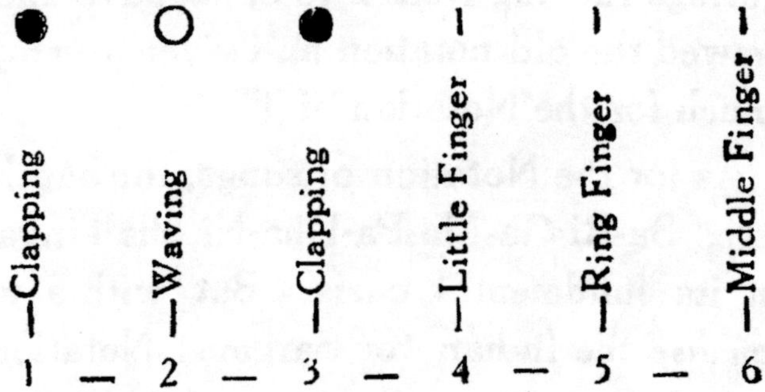

Take again a North Indian Thala, Chowthal. It consists of 4 clappings, 6 fingerings, and 2 wavings—in all 12 aksharas which may be represented thus :—

●	I	I	I	●	I	I	I	●	O	●	O
Clapping	Little Finger	Ring Finger	Middle Finger	Clapping	Little Finger	Ring Finger	Middle Finger	Clapping	Waving	Clapping	Waving
1	2	3	4	5	6	7	8	9	10	11	12

As the student learns each new thala, he may easily get it analysed into clappings, fingerings and wavings and have such analysis recorded in the manner indicated above. The old notation of I to denote *Laghu* and o to denote *Drutha* has a deal of ambiguity and confusion about it, especially to a beginner. For instance, the Laghu-sign I stands for one clapping and any number of fingerings ranging from 2 tò 8. I have therefore eschewed the old notation and given you my own. So much for the Notation of Thala.

As for the Notation of songs, the Sapthaswaras, *viz.*, Sa-Ri-Ga-Ma-Pa-Dha-Ni, shall invariably form its fundmental basis. But with a view to *nationalise* the Indian (or Sargam) Notation from Mount to Cape, those Sapthaswaras shall invariably be written in Nagari characters. The *Sahithyam* or wording of songs may be written in the language of those songs or in any other language; but the Sargam Notation of those songs must be uniformly written in Nagari, throughout the length and breadth of India. The music students need not fear that they have to learn, for this purpose, Sanskrit Language. I assure them that it is enough for them to learn seven letters—not more nor less than seven letters—of the seven notes of the scale. They are as follows:—

Notes	Nagari Letters		Same Letters but Conjunct	
	Short	Long	Short	Long
Sa	स	सा	स्स	स्सा
Ri	रि	री	रिं	रीं
Ga	ग	गा	ग्ग	ग्गा
Ma	म	मा	म्म	म्मा
Pa	प	पा	प्प	प्पा
Dha	ध	धा	ध्ध	ध्धा
Ni	नि	नी	न्नि	न्नी

With the sapthaswaras written in Nagari characters, we have yet to learn some special signs to denote pitch, time-value, commencement, end, repetition, grouping, rest, and so forth. Let us study them one by one.

The signs of Pitch may be as follows :—

Pitch	Signs	Signs Explained	Example
High or Thara Sthayi	· over a line	A Dot above	सं
Middle or Madhayama Sthayi	Nil	Nil	स
Lower or Mandra Sthayi	· under a line	A Dot below	स

N.B.—Whatever applies to स applies equally to each of the other six swaras.

The signs of Time-Value may be as follows :—

Time Value	Signs	Signs Explained	Examples
Ekamathra	Nil	Nil	स
Ardhamathra	—	A Single Horizontal Line below.	सरि
Chathurthamathra	— —	A Double Horizontal Line below.	सारिगम
Ashtamamathra	— — — —	A Quadruple Horizontal Line below	सरिगमपधनिस

N.B.—Whatever applies to स applies equally to each of the other six swaras. Be it noted here that the European signs, Crotchet, Quaver, Semiquaver and Demisemiquaver correspond respectively to Ekamathra, Ardhamattra, Chathurthamattra and Ashtamamattra.

The following supplementary signs have also to he studied :—

What the Signs indicate	Signs	Remarks if any
Commencement ...	●	
End ...	॥	
Drone ...	ऽ	
Rest ...	—	
Ditto ...	,,	
Grouping ...	⌒	
Accent ...	W	
Repetition ...	+	
Portion Repeated ...	+{ }	
Prolongation of the previous Vowel sound.	———	This will occur only in Sahitya and not in Notation.
Komala ...	रि$_1$	So is the case with each of ग-म-ध-नि
Thivra ...	रि$_2$	
Suddha Gandhara ..	(रि$_2$) ग	See *infra*
Shadsruthi Rishabha ...	(ग$_1$) रि	
Sudha Nishada ...	(ध$_2$) नि	
Shadsruthi Dhaivatha ...	(नि$_1$) ध	
Anuswara ...	(गस) स	Ex :—सरिगसस (गस)

At the commencement of a song, the Mela, the Raga, the Thala, the Kala, the Gathi, the Arohana and the Avarohana should be clearly given. The flat or sharp notes should also be pointed out. It flat, write, for example, रि$_1$; if sharp, write रि$_2$; and so on with each of —ग—म—ध – नि as well. Re nember again that the theory of flat and sharp notes applies only to रि—ग—म—ध—नि and never to स—प. Remember also that 1 and 2, indicating flat and sharp notes respectively, will be tacked on to any of the former but not to either of the latter.

At this stage, I may be confronted with a query, whether, in view of the fact* that Venkatamakhi gave 16 names to 12 swaras, the nomenclature of Komala and Thivra and their respective signs 1 and 2 cover all the "16 Swaras" ; and whether, if not, what special signs have been, or should be, given to the four special swaras of the Karnatic System, *viz.*, Suddha Gandhara, Shadsruthi Rishabha, Suddha Nishada, and Shadsruthi Dhaivatha.

---

* Vide my *Theory of Music.*

In the following Figure,

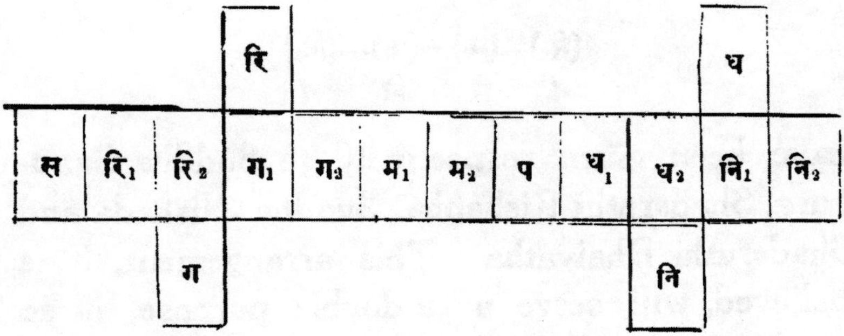

the four side-swaras, so to speak, marked रि-ग-ध-नि belong exclusively to the Karnatic System and are of Venkatamakhi's creation, for all practical purposes; while, the twelve Swaras, marked स—रि$_1$—रि$_2$—ग$_1$—ग$_2$—म$_1$—म$_2$—प—ध$_1$—ध$_2$—नि$_1$—नि$_2$ form a common feature of both the Indian (North and South) and the European systems. Signs like रि$_1$—रि$_2$—रि$_3$ to indicate respectively Suddha Rishabha, Chathusrithi Rishabha and Shadsruthi Rishabha will not only clash with the general arrangement, hitherto followed, but also prevent us from ariving at a notatin *common* to our country as a whole. Reference has already been made in my *Theory of Music* that Suddha Gandhara and Chathusruthi Rishabha sound alike; as also Sadharana Gandhara and Shadsruthi Rishabha, Suddha Nishada and Chathusruthi Dhaivatha, and Kaisiki Nishada and Shadsruthi Dhaivatha. Hence the signs

(रि$_2$)—(ग$_1$)—(ध$_2$)—(नि$_1$)
ग रि नि ध

have been given respectively to Suddha Gandhara, Shadsruthi Rishabha, Suddha Nishada and Shadsruthi Dhaivatha. This arrangement, it is believed, will serve us a double purpose, in so much as it avoids clashing with the arrangement in other systems of music and indicates the true nature of the sounds of the four special swaras of the Karnatic System. The Kanakangi scale may, for example, be writen thus:—

(रि$_2$) (ध$_2$)
स—रि$_1$—गं—म$_1$—प—ध$_1$—नि—स

I shall bring this subject of Sargam Notation to a close with giving you a few typical exercises for practice, only to familiarise you with all the signs and explanations mentioned above.

TYPICAL EXERCISES.

Caution—The teacher should demonstrate to the pupils how to sound त (tha)— क (ka) in Vilambitha (slow), Madhyama (middle) and Drutha (quick) Kalas. Later on, the very swara letters should be taught to be sung; instead of त—क in all the three Kalas. Then the pupils should be slowly initiated into the saralis* and their paraphernalia, till they reach the classical songs.

* Rightly, *Swaravalis.*

EXERCISE I.

SOME PHRASES AND IDIOMS,

● त—क	त—क	। त—क	। त—क	● त—क	○ त—क	● त—क	○ त—क
स रि	ग म	प ध	नि सं	सं नि	ध प	म ग	रि स
सरि सरि	सरि गम	सरि गम	पध निसं	संनि संनि	संनि धप	संनि धप	मग रिस
स रि	सरि गम	प ध	पध निसं	सं नि	संनि धप	म ग	मग रिस
स रिं	सरिगम पम	प ध	पधनिसं रिंसं	सं नि	संनिधप मप	म ग	प्रमगरि गस

सरि	गरि	गम	गम	पंम	पध	पध	निस	सनि	धनि	धप	धप	मप	मग	मग	रिस
साऽ	ऽरि	ग	म	पाऽ	ऽध	नि	स	साऽ	ऽनि	ध	प	माऽ	ऽग	रि	स
साऽ	ऽरि	गम	गरि	गाऽ	ऽम	पध ,	निस	सांऽ	ऽनि	धप	धनि	धाऽ	ऽप	मग	रिस
सऱी	ऽग	मग	रिस	रिगा	ऽम	पध	निसं	सं'नी	ऽध	पध	निसं	निधा	ऽप	मग	रिस
स	री	ऽग	म	प	धा	ऽनि	सं	सं	नीं	ऽध	प	म	गा	ऽरि	स
साऽ	ऽरी	गम	पम	प	धा	ऽनि	सं	साऽ	नि	धनि	धप	म	गा	ऽरि	स

●	I	I	I	●	○	●	○
त—क	त—क	त—क	त—क	त—क	त—क	त—क	त—क
सी ढग	मग रिग	पधा डनि	*सरि *स	*सनी डध	संरि सानि	धमा ढग	रिग स
सग री	सरि गम	पाडधनि धाढनिस	निडसरि *सा	संध नी	सं'नि धप	माडपम गाढमग	रीढगरि सा
सरि गम	गरि गम	पम गम	पध *निस	सं'नि धप	धनि धप	मप धप	मग रिस
सारि गम	प *सा	डरि *सनि	सां ड	सं'नि धप	म धा	ढग रिग	सा ढ

स री	ड री	ड सनि	सरिगम पधनिसं	सं नी	ड नी	ड सं रिं	सनिधप मगरिस
सा ड	ड री	ड ग	मपधनि सां	सां ड	ड नी	ड ध	पमगरि सा
साडरिग रिग	गस रिग	मपा डधा	डनि सं	सांडनिध धनि	निप सनि	धमा डगा	डरि सा

EXERCISE II.

HEADING.

Mala 29. Dira Sankarabharanam			
	Thala	...	Adi.
	Kala	...	Madyama.
	Gathi	...	Chathusra.

Arohana — स रि$_2$ ग$_2$ म$_1$ प ध$_2$ नि$_2$ सं.,

Avarohana — सं नि$_2$ ध$_2$ प म$_1$ ग$_2$ रि$_2$ स.

Pallavi.

श्री म ही शू र पु रा धी श.

Anupallavi.

चामुण्डादेवीपरिपालित साम्राज्यसार्वभौम.

Swaram.	*Sahithyam,*
सां-संरिं-संनिधप-धनि-धाप-मगम-	श्रीकृष्णइवसर्वमतसाम्यसुन्वित्त,
पा-पध-पपमग-मप-माग-रिगम-	श्रीरामवत्पदचरततार, चतु-
सारिगा-मपध-मापधां-निसंरिं-	र्वेदवेदांगसारज्ञ. विश्ववि-
सां-रिंगंरिं-सांसंधा-गंरीं-संसंध-	द्यानिलयस्थापक, सदाचार-
रिं रिं रिं-संसंध-रिं रिं-संसंध-रिंसंनि-धनि-	सदयहृदय नगरपरिष्कार-
पा-धनि-संरिंगंसां-रिंगंमांगं-	निरत, नंजुण्डेशकठाक्षाः
पंमंगं-गंरिंसं-संनिधनि-संमंगंरिं-संनि-	भवतः श्रियमभिपुष्णन्तु,
धरिं-संनिंध-पधनिसां-मपा-धनि-	सहजप्रियाश्रितसुजनशुभकर,
सं-गमपधनि- (श्री)	कर्णाटजनपदमण्डन- (श्री)

Charanam.

राजेन्द्र भोतव्यम् श्रीकृष्ण.

Swaram

1

सा-नी-री-गामधा गेगपा-
सारिगा-म- (रा)

2

रिरींग-सरिग-मम्माग-रिगम-
पणाम-गमप-धध्धा-संध-
धमगसा-रिगम- (रा)

3

गाम-रींग-सारि-गाम-दाध-
नारिं-गांमं-गांरिं-मानि-धाप-
माग-सा-रिगम- (रा)

4

मम्मप-मगरिग-
मम्मध-पमगरि-
मम्मनि-धपमग
मम्मप-संनिध-
धमन्म-समम- (रा)

5

पपप-सांसं-धध-रींरिं-
नि रीं-निरि-गंमंगंरिंसं.
सं-निसंनिधपा-म-
गमगरिसा-ग-मधमंरिग-
सगपसां-मंगांरिं-संनिधनि-
रिं सांसं-पंध-पमग-सगम- (रा)

Sahithyam.

1

अस्मद्देशीयगांधर्ववेदं
मवीमि- (रा)

2

शारंगरचितसंगीतसमय
पारंगतमखिनीराजित
जनपदः सोऽयम्- (रा)

3

गीतशास्त्रमीदृशंतुश्रीकृष्णेन
नाहामित्यनेकधास्तुतं हि
सारमतेः (रा)

4

सर्वतइहपुरा
सर्वनृपतिभिः
सर्वरसविततं
सर्वदाऽभ्यस्तं हि
सुगुण- (रा)

5

सकलरोगहरंसर्वसुकर्मसु
निरवधिकोत्साहकरणं
आपिचपरमात्म
भजनसुखकरं सरूपतांच
वितरति ; अतःखलुसकल
जनन्नुतं- (रा)

6

धनिध-धा-निधप-मध-
पमगरी-गगपा-री-गमपा
सा-रिगम-नी-सरिग-सा-
रिगम पधनि-सांरिं -
गंमंगंरिं -संसंसं-संधा-पम-
गमप-धपा-पमगसा-
रिगम- (रा)

7

नीसं-धनि-पधनि-संनिधप-
संध-पमंगरि-गमपा-धनिपा-
धनिसां-गांरिं संनि-
संरिं -गंसंगंरिं-नि-
संगंरिं-मंगंरिं सां-निरिंसं-संनिधप-
मधप-पमगसा-रिगम- (रा)

8

सां-रिंसंनि-धंनि-पंधनि-
संनीधप-मध-पमगरि-
गमपा-निपा-धनि-
संसंरिं-संसंरिं-संनि-
धधनि-धधनि-धप-
सधां-रिंसां-गंरिं-मंगां रिं -संसंनि
संारिं-गंमंगां-नीसं रिंगंरीं
धानि-संरिंसां-सांनि-धनिपा-संनि
सांरिंगरि-निरि-गंमंगरि-
संनि-संगंरीं-संनिध-
धधनी-धपम-पधपा-मंगं-रिगम- (रा)

6

अहह सांप्रतमिदंखमगमद-
तितरांदीनदशां रागलय-
भावगतिहीन गातृजनगीतं
कलुषितं ; समस्तजनार्तिदं
अभवदहो सकलभूप-
सुत- (रा)

7

श्रीसिटलिसुखनिखिलजन
पदमुविपरिकलयंत्ववदसीय-
दशां ; दारिद्र्यंहिपरमदु:खदं
निदानं ; किंबहुना
वर्धतेगानबीजंनृपत्यंमसा
सततं- (रा)

8

नूनमिदमवनिपति
महादरत उपचयमनुरमं
भजेत हि
पगानिानित्रगनर
विटलसुमखिमुख
कलावतांकलायथा
टस्कानि-व-
वेरियखडिष्चतंजप्र-
देशवसुधाऽधीश्वरपारिग्रहात्
श्रीरामदासकलित
संगीतामिगमक्षेमाय भवतोत्रिना गतिःक? ()

NOTATION

●	1	1	1	●	○	●	○
त—क	त—क	त—क	त—क	त—क	त—क	त—क	त—क
			Pallavi.				
	*						(नीप)
	+ { सां	संध संनि	पा ऽ	मा ऽप	मग पम	पा धनि	पा धनि
	श्री	म ———	ही ———	श ——— र	पु ———	ता ———	——— धी ———
संनि संध	धनि }						
——— ——— श	——— }						

●	I	I	I	◐	○	●	○
त—क	त—क	त—क	त—क	त—क	त—क	त—क	त—क
			Anupallavi.				
	+ { सां चा	संध पम ज्ञ ——	गरि गमा —— ब्हा	ऽम गम —दे ——	पा धनि धी—— प—	पा धनि —— रि—	संनि सां पा ——
धाऽनिसं निप लि —— त	धनि } ,, —— } ,,	,, ,, ,, ,,	,, ,, ,, ,,	,, ,, ,, ,,	,, ,, ,, ,,	,, ,, ,, ,,	,, संरिं ,, ——
गारिं संनि	,, सारिं	गमं पमं	गामं रींगं	सांनि संग	री ऽसं	निसं धाऽनिस	विप धनि
लि —त—	—— सा	——— —	भ्रा ——	व्य—— सा	—— वं	—— भौ—	म ——

Swara Sahithyam

सां	सांरिं	संनि	धप	धनि	धा	पम	गम	पा	पध	पप	मग	मप	मा	गरि	गम
श्री	कृष्ण	द्रुव	सर्व	मत	सा	न्युसु	चित्त	श्री	रा—	मव	त्पद	चर	त —	त्पर	चतु
सा	रिगा	ऽम	पध	मा	पधा	ऽनि	संरिं	सां	रिंगं	रिंसां	ऽसं	धा	गंरिं	ऽसं	संध
वें	देव	दां ——	ग	सा	रज्ञ	—	विश्ववि	धा	निल	यस्था	— प	क —	सदा	— चा	— र
रिंरिं	रिंसं	संध	रिं रिं	संसं	धरिं	सनि	धनि	पा	ऽध	निसं	रिंगं	सा	ऽरिं	गंमां	ऽगं
सद	यहृ	दय	नग	रप	रिष्का	—र	निर	त	—नं	जुण्डे	—श	क	—टा	—क्षा	:
पंमं	गंगं	रिंसं	संनि	धनि	संमं	गंरिं	संनि	धरिं	संनि	धंप	धनि	सां	ऽम	प:	धनि
भव	तःश्रि	यम	भिपु	ण्णन्तु	सह	जांघ्रि	या—	श्रित	सुज	नश्च	भक	र———	क	र्णा	ढज
संग	मप	धनि	}	(श्री)											
नप	मद	ण्ढन													

⊛	1	1	1	●	○	●	○
त—क	त—क	त—क	त—क	त—क	त—क	त—क	त—क
			Charanam.				
	*	(पम्मा)				(मपा)	
	पप	मा S	मग धम	पा S	S मग	पा S	मध पम
	रा—	जं ——	———	न्द्र ———	——— श्रो	———	त — व्यं
(गल)							
सा सरि	गम ,,	,, ,,	,, ,,	,, ,,	,, मप	धनि संनि	धप मध
श्री कृ—	ष्ण ,,	,, ,,	,, ,,	,, ,,	,, श्रो	———	त— व्यं
पम गरि	गम ,,	,, ,,	,, ,,	,, ,,	,, ,,	,, संरिं	संनि धप
श्री— कृ	ष्ण ,,	,, ,,	,, ,,	,, ,,	,, ,,	,, ———	त — व्यं

मग	सरि	गम	,,	,,	,,	,,	,,	,,	,,	,,	मग	पा	ऽ	मप	पम
श्री	कृ—	ष्ण	,,	,,	,,	,,	,,	,,	,,	,,	श्री	———		त	ध्यं
						1									
* सा	ऽ	ऽ	नी	ऽ	री		गा	ऽम	धा	ऽ	री	ऽग	पा	ऽ	सा
अ ——		——स्म		———	हे	——	श्री	य ——	गा	——	न्थ	—वं	वे	——	हं
ऽ	रिगा	ऽम	(रा)												
——	ब्रवी	-मि													
						2									
रि	रींऽ	गस	रिग	म	म्माऽ	गारि	गम	प	प्पाऽ	मग	मप	ध	ध्धा	सध	पम
शा	रं—	गर	चित	सं	गी—	तस	मय	पा	रं—	गत	मखि	नी	रा	जित	जन
गसा	ऽरि	गम	(रा)												
पदः	सो	ऽयम													

●	।	।	।	●	○	●	○
त—क	त—क	त—क	त—क	त—क	त—क	त—क	त—क
			3				
गाऽ मरी	ऽग साऽ	रिगा ऽम	पाऽ धनी	ऽरिं गाऽ	मगा ऽरिं	साऽ निधा	ऽप माऽ
गी तशा	स्त्र मी	दृशं तु	श्री कृष्णे	न ना	हमि त्य	ने कथा	स्तु तं
गसा ऽरि	गम } (रा)						
हिसा र	मंते						
			4				
म म्मप	मग रिग	म म्मध	पम गारि	म म्मनि	धप मग	म म्मध	संनि धध
स वंत	इह पुरा	स वेन्द्र	पति भिः	स वैर	सवि ततं	स वैदा	——ऽभ्य

म म्मस	मन } (रा)						
स्तं हिसु	गुण						
			5				
पप पसां	ऽसं धध	रीं रिंनि	रीं निरिं	गंमं गंरिं	सां मं	निसं निध	पा म
सक लरो—	—ग हरं	स वैद्व	क मैंसु	निर वधि	को ——	त्साह कर	णं ——अ
गम गरि	सा ग	मध मरि	गस गप	सां मंगां	ऽरिं संनि	धनि रिंसां	ऽसं संध
पिच पर	मा त्म	भज मसु	लक रंस	क पतां	—च वित	रति अतः	म लुस
पम गस	गम } (रा)						
कल जन	मुतं						

●	I	I	I	●	○	●	○
त—क	त—क	त—क	त—क	त—क	त—क	त—क	त—क
			6				
धनि धधा	ऽनि धध	मध पम	गारि गम	परी ऽग	मप सा	रिग मनी	ऽस रिग
अह हसां	—प्र तमि	वंस मग	मद् तित	रांदी — न	इमां रा	गल यभा	व गति
सा ऽरिं	गम पध	निसां ऽरिं	गंमं गंरिं	संसं संसं	धा पम	गम पध	पा षम
ही न	गा— तृज	नगी — तं	कलु षितं	सम स्तज	ना र्तिद	मम वद	हो सक
गसा ऽरिं	गम } (रा)						
लभू ——प	तुत						

7

नी	संध	निध	धनि	संनि	धप	संध	पम	गरि	गम	धा	धनि	पा	धनि	सां	ऽगा
ग्री	सिट	लिड्ड	लनि	खिल	जन	पद	श्रुवि	परि	कल	यं	त्वद	सी	यद	शां	दा
ऽरिं	संनि	संरिं	गंसं	गरिं	निसं	गंरिं	मंगं	रिंसां	ऽनि	रिंसं	संनि	धपा	ऽम	धप	मप
रि	द्रयहि	पर	मड्ढः	खदं	निद्रा	—नं	किंव	द्रुना	व	वैते	गा	नंनी	अं	नृप	स्यं—
गसा	ऽरि	गम	(रा)												
भेसा	स	ततं													

●	|	|	|	●	○	●	○
त—क	त—क	त—क	त—क	त—क	त—क	त—क	त—क
			8				
सां ऽरि	संनि धनि	पध निसं	नी धप	मध पम	गरि गम	पा ऽनि	पा धनि
नू न	मिद मव	निप तिम	हा हर	तउ पच	यम नुप	मं भ	जे तहि
सस रिंसं	संरिं संनि	धध निध	धनि धप	संधा ऽरिं	मां गरीं	ऽमं गां	रिंसं संनि
पग निनि	वग नर	विट लसु	मखि मुख	कला व	तां कला	—य था	ठस्क निब
सारिं गंमं	गां ऽ	नीसं रिंगं	रीं ऽ	धानि संरिं	सा ऽ	सांनि धनि	पा संनि
वेरि या	खं——	डिञ्च तंज	प——	देश वसु	धा——	धीश्र रप	रि ग्रहाद्

सांरिं	गांरिं	निरिं	गंमं	गांरिं	सांनि	सांगं	रीं	ऽसं	निध	पध	धी	ऽधं	पम	पध	पा
भी—	रा—	म—	धा—	सक	कित	सं—	गी	त	निग	म—	श्रे	—मा	—य	मव	तो
ऽम	गरि	गम (रा)													
—वि	नाग	तिःक													

EXERCISE IV.

C. Major. (*S*ankarabharanam.)

Thala—Adi ; **Kala**—Madhyama ; **Gathi**—Thisra.

N,B,—Only Notes and no wording.

●	I	I	I	●	○	●	○
त-क-त	त-क-त	त-क-त	त-क-त	त-क-त	त-क-त	त-क-त	त-क-त
प-म-म	ध-म-म	स-म-प	धा-ह-ह	नि-प-ध	सं-प-प	म-प-ध	मा-ह-ह
प-स-धानि	सा-निध-पम	प-ध-मप	ध-मग-रिग	सग-म-गम	प-पध-निध	प-सं-मम	धनि-सां-ह

रि-सं-रिं	संरि-सनि-धनि	*स-नि-स*	रिंस-निध-निसं	रि-स-रि	सरि-सनि-धनि	सं-नि-सं	रिम-निध-पम
मगं-रिं-सं-मां	गम-गं-मं-गं-रि	संनि-धप-म	ड-ड-ड	सरि-गम-पध	निसं-रिग-मा	गरिं-मंगंरिस	रिसं-निध-पम